JOURNAL *of* MUSEUM EDUCATION

VOLUME 34 ❧ NUMBER 2 ❧ SUMMER 2009

A PUBLICATION OF THE MUSEUM EDUCATION ROUNDTABLE

Educational Leadership

Cover: A John G. Shedd Aquarium educator leads a guest through a hands-on animal encounter with a Black and White Argentine Tegu to educate and inspire the guest to make a positive impact on the environment. *Courtesy © Shedd Aquarium/Heidi Zeiger.*

ISBN 978-1-59874-821-5

First published 2009 by Left Coast Press, Inc.

Published 2016 by Routledge
2 Park Square, Milton Park, Abingdon, Oxon OX14 4RN
711 Third Avenue, New York, NY 10017

Routledge is an imprint of the Taylor and Francis Group, an informa business

Production and Composition by Detta Penna, Penna Design, Abbotsford, British Columbia

ISBN 13: 978-1-59874-821-5 (pbk)

The other day I was talking with my museum's educator, Olga Peterfalvy, about her efforts to identify and reach out to potential, new audiences. She writes and edits a blog on the museum web site (see http://www.crime-museum.org/blog/) as well as coordinates educational programs. We talked about introducing new technological strategies to her outreach arsenal including Youtube videos, podcasts, and other tools. It occurred to me that this was *not* the kind of discussion that I had with my supervisor when I started my museum education career 17 years ago at Colonial Williamsburg. It was not that we neglected outreach, it was just on a much different scale. A single educator could not reach tens of thousands of people and never would she have been expected to. Today, Olga is developing skills in marketing, technology, and even sales. The profession has changed.

Museum educators occupy a unique position in that they have both the understanding of how visitors learn as well as subject matter knowledge for their museum specialties. Because educators are also reflexive learners, they are creative and innovative and tend to be flexible when faced with change. However, in order to be successful in a difficult economy and adapt to the changing workplace, members of our profession also need to demonstrate that they have the skills and abilities to lead in the field. The divisions between museum departments are beginning to blur and even overlap. It is imperative to show that we are nimble enough to take on new roles and responsibilities within the museum as those opportunities arise, whatever they might be.

This issue of the *Journal of Museum Education* examines the leadership roles that museum educators assume both within their institutions and the museum field. The Guest Editor, Tina Nolan, advises us of what museum educators should know and be able to do, and in doing so she argues the need for the profession to establish a standard. The issue envisions a future for what we want the profession to be and articulates strategies for how to achieve it. Because the field demands it, educators will develop new skills and volunteer to assume increased responsibility. . . like Olga.

Liz Maurer

Elizabeth L. Maurer is the Director of Operations for the National Museum of Crime & Punishment in Washington, DC.

JOURNAL of MUSEUM EDUCATION

A PUBLICATION OF THE MUSEUM EDUCATION ROUNDTABLE

Editor
ELIZABETH MAURER
Director of Operations
The National Museum of Crime & Punishment

Educational Leadership
Guest Editor
TINA NOLAN
Associate Director of Partnerships, National College of Education,
National-Louis University

Editorial Advisors

AMELIA CHAPMAN, Curator of Education, Pacific Asia Museum

CYNTHIA COPELAND, Principal, The OutSourced Muse

MARIA DEL CARMEN COSSU, International Arts and Early Childhood Education,
Smithsonian Early Enrichment Center

MARK HOWELL, Director of Education, American Civil War Center at Historic Tredegar

LYNN MCRAINEY, Director of Education, Chicago History Museum

LAURA ROBERTS, Director of the Boston Center for Adult Education and
principal at Roberts Consultant, Strategic Thinking for Cultural Nonprofits

SUSAN SPERO, Associate Professor, Museum Studies, John F. Kennedy University

The Museum Education Roundtable (MER) is a nonprofit organization based in Washington, DC, dedicated to enriching and promoting the field of Museum Education. Through publications, programs, and communication networks, MER fosters professionalism, encourages leadership, scholarship, and research in museum-based learning, and advocates the inclusion and application of museum-based learning in the general education arena. For more information on MER and its activities, please contact via email at info@mer-online.com, or on the web at www.mer-online.org. Members receive the Journal of Museum Education as a benefit of membership. Write to MER at PO Box 15727, Washington, DC 20003.

The Museum Educator Crisis

Tina R. Nolan

January 15, 2009: "Zoo Feels Bite of Rough Economy," *Chicago Tribune*

February 13, 2009: "Children's Museum Cutting Staff, Pay, Hours," *Daily Herald*

March 13, 2009: "NYC's Metropolitan Museum to Lay Off 74 More People," *Daily Herald*

April 10, 2009: "Corcoran Gallery Lays Off 18 Employees," *The Washington Post*

June 22, 2009: "Metropolitan Museum of Art Completes Round of Layoffs," *New York Times*

The picture is clear: museums have taken a hit in the current economic recession, and so far there does not seem to be an end in sight. A recent Museum Research Associates survey shows that museum educators comprise the largest segment of museum staff to lose their jobs in this current financial crisis.[1] How did museum educators find themselves in this position? Do museum leaders think educators are dispensable? I would argue that a growing identity crisis among museum educators lies at the heart of their current vulnerability and that their identity crisis was brought about in part by the release of one of the landmark documents in recent museum history.

The American Association of Museums (AAM) Report, *Excellence and Equity: Education and the Public Dimension of Museums* issued the following as its first principle recommendation, "Assert that museums place education in the broadest sense of the word at the center of their public service role."[2] The report offers clearly articulated strategies related to learning, interpretation, scholarship, collaboration, and professional development. The third edition of this seminal document was released in 2008 virtually unchanged from the original version released in 1992. The AAM Task Force on Museum Education that wrote *Excellence and Equity* was right when they argued that education was the purview of the entire museum. They were right when they called for museums to dedicate themselves to public service. Museum educators, however, did not position themselves well to lead the way toward expanding the role of museums as "educational institutions without boundaries."[3] By re-orienting the museum around its educational mission, the expertise of educators was distributed to other departments such as audience research, exhibits, and public relations. This is not at all a bad thing; in fact, it is exactly what the authors intended. They argued that "the educational role involved the entire museum — from trustees to guards in the galleries, from public relations staff to docents who give tours, from curators, to educators."[4] Instead of playing a leadership role in building the capacity of others to do this work, the job of the average museum educator became blurred with customer service. They often became front line staff instead of highly valued resources in achieving a new public dimension for their museums. In larger institutions, museum educators handed over the responsibility for collecting data on visitor learning to other departments or outside consultants — further marginalizing themselves in the process. We are left with well-intentioned museum educators who feel undervalued, unclear of where they fit within the larger museum context, and who come and go from our institutions. The profession as a whole is dichotomous with no common language, no consistent set of practices, and few educational leaders.

It is time to look at the future of museum educators through a new lens. Doing so will require a deep understanding of its current state, a clear vision of the best possible future for the profession, and a strong set of recommendations for how to achieve that new vision.

Thankfully, previous editions of the *Journal of Museum Education* have articulated the current state of the profession. In the Spring 2006 edition of the *Journal*, Gail Anderson argued that today's museums lack relevance because they continue to look inward when planning for the future. "If museums are to succeed as public institutions," she wrote, "they must instead look outward to partner with their community to address issues such as equity and diversity, the role of museums as educational institutions, and community engagement."[5] Mary Ellen Munley and Randy Roberts suggested that museum educators must play the role of institutional change agents, increasing the public value of their institutions by positioning themselves as "the critical point of connection between the community and the museum."[6] Elsa Bailey explored the subject in depth in the Fall 2006 edition entitled *The Professional Relevance of Museum Educators*. Bailey's edition of the *Journal* described in detail the current state of the museum education profession from the circuitous routes museum educators take to enter the field, to how they learn their craft, to what keeps them there.[7]

In this edition of the *Journal*, we have taken deliberate steps to draw on what we already know about the current state, and we urge museum educators to refer back to the original intent of *Excellence and Equity* as we raise the central question that faces us: *What will it take to reposition museum educators from the margins of our institutions to the center?* We provide a new orientation to educational leadership, a topic rarely discussed among the museum educator profession, and have organized the articles around the following set of questions:

- Why and how must museum education departments change, and who can affect such change?

- What should a museum education department leader know and be able to do in order to affect change?

- What are the ramifications of change leadership for the rest of the institution?

Rafael Rosa opens the dialogue by highlighting specific voices that represent the future of the profession: those on the front lines who feel undervalued or unprepared for the leadership positions they have assumed or aspire to assume. Leslie Bedford continues the conversation begun in 2006 by inviting Mary Ellen Munley, Randy Roberts, Brigid Globensky, and Elsa Bailey to describe the future of the profession as they see it. Mary Kay Cunningham explores the envisioned future, focusing specifically on the leadership competencies and strategies needed to achieve this vision. Knowing that what we were creating was theoretical, we felt it necessary to include real world examples of current leadership strategies and recommendations from new leaders in the field and provide a set of recommended literature for building a foundation in educational leadership. In the final article, I issue a call to action for current and aspiring leaders to assume a new role as change leaders for the museum education profession.

The world is changing rapidly, and many of the old ways of doing business are not easily adapted to today's circumstances. John Falk and Beverly Sheppard's book, *Thriving in the Knowledge Age*, attests to this very notion:

> At a time when many people all over the world feel that their core institutions are failing them, we should be increasingly attuned to the dramatic changes taking place in society. The familiarity of an Industrial Age, the time in which museums as we know them were born, is yielding to the new challenges of a Knowledge Age. No institution, however cherished, will be untouched by the economic, social, and political changes that are sweeping old ways aside.[8]

Falk and Sheppard's book was published in 2006, well before the American economy entered into recession. The new reality is playing itself out now in the lives of our colleagues; the ones who have lost their jobs and the ones who have been left behind to do more with considerably less. And with such change comes a golden opportunity. It is in *this* moment in our history that museum educators can help to reshape not only their profession, but also the future of the relationship between the public and its cultural institutions. Museum educators can and should play a critical role in shaping the future of museums in America, but they will require leaders who understand their role as change agents. These new educational leaders must pioneer new practices, advocate in new ways for their staffs, and come together to articulate a new role and a consistent identity for the museum educators they serve.

Acknowledgments

Special thanks to the many current and aspiring leaders I've encountered in my research: To Mary Kay Cunningham, Mark Larson, Susan Spero, and Linda Tafel for sharing their wisdom and experience; to the NLU doctoral program advisory board members: David Ebitz , Erik Holland, Cheryl Mell, Lynn McRainey, Kate Meyer, Linell Monson-Lasswell, Ted Purinton, Gerri Spinella, Treenan Sturman, and Lynn Uyen Tran. And heartfelt thanks to Kevin and Bridget Nolan for their ongoing support and to my parents for inspiring in me a love of museums and adventure.

Notes

1. Ron Kley reports that as many as 60% of the total staff cuts/freezes reported as of March 15, 2009 came from the ranks of museum education. See Kley's article in this issue.
2. American Association of Museums, *Excellence and Equity: Education and the Public Dimension of Museums* (Washington, DC: 1992), 8.
3. American Association of Museums, 2.
4. American Association of Museums, 4.
5. Gail Anderson, "Museums and Relevancy," *Journal of Museum Education* 31, no.1 (Spring 2006).
6. Mary Ellen Munley and Randy Roberts, "Are Museum Educators Still Necessary?," *Journal of Museum Education* 31, no.1 (Spring 2006): 36.
7. Elsa Bailey, "Researching Museum Educators' Perceptions of their Roles, Identity, and Practice," *Journal of Museum Education* 31, no.3 (Fall 2006): 175-197.
8. John H. Falk and Beverly K. Sheppard, *Thriving in the Knowledge Age: New Business Models for Museums and Other Cultural Institutions* (Lanham, MD: Alta Mira Press, 2006): viii.

Tina Nolan (Tina.Nolan@nl.edu) has spent the past 16 years working as an educator in cultural institutions. In February 1999, Nolan helped to open the Chicago Academy of Sciences Peggy Notebaert Nature Museum. In 2000, Nolan was Manager of Student and Teacher Programs, and was named Director of Education at the Nature Museum in 2001. Nolan joined National-Louis University in 2006 as Associate Director of Partnerships in the National College of Education. In this capacity, Nolan establishes new partnerships between NLU's National College of Education and school districts, education reform organizations, cultural institutions and community organizations nationally and internationally. Nolan is also an adjunct faculty member at National-Louis University and is currently teaching graduate-level coursework in the Educational Leadership program. Nolan continues to work with museums and other not-for-profit educational organizations as an independent education consultant. Most recently, Nolan became a board member for the Museum Education Roundtable. Nolan has a Masters degree in Educational Leadership and is currently pursuing a doctorate in Education where the focus of her research is on educational leadership in cultural institutions.

Recessionary Layoffs in Museum Education
Survey Results and Implications

Ron Kley

Abstract   A recent survey of recession-driven museum staff reductions suggests the possible loss of tens of thousands of museum personnel nationwide and identifies educators as among those most severely impacted. Survey findings are summarized, and the implications for both affected personnel and downsized institutions are considered.

As a co-chair of the New England Museum Association's professional affinity group for Independent Museum Professionals, I had been assigned the role of "lead-off batter" for a day-long workshop designed to provide a very basic introduction to independent consulting/contracting work for the benefit of museum staff members recently laid off as a consequence of recessionary cutbacks in institutional budgets.

Having heard of many such layoffs "through the grapevine," but recognizing that that the plural of anecdote is not data, I decided to take a stab at data collection via the Internet, using the free survey generation and tabulation capabilities available through the web site of SurveyMonkey.com.

By all rights, it seemed as if such a survey initiative should have been sponsored by one or another of the regional or national museum service organizations, but, finding no evidence of such an effort having been undertaken, I announced my own modest survey through several museum listservs on March 1, 2009 and hoped that some real data might be collected. Although I asked respondents to identify their institutions and to provide their e-mail addresses if they wished to receive a summary of survey data, I assured them that I would not name any individual institutions in any such summaries and that respondents' identities would also be treated as confidential.

Journal of Museum Education, Volume 34, Number 2, Summer 2009, pp. 123-128.

In just over two weeks' time, 99 responses had been received from 30 states and the Province of Ontario. The most numerous responses were from California and New York (11 each), Massachusetts (10), and New Mexico and Virginia (7 each). The institutions represented included organizations of just about every imaginable type and size from tiny local historical societies to major government operated institutions.

Surprisingly (or so I thought), given the fact that this was specifically identified as a survey of "Museum Staff Recessionary Cutbacks," there were 17 institutions that reported no staff losses. One, in fact, reported that a single position had been added in 2008 and that there were still optimistic plans to add four more positions in 2009.

On balance, the reports were more sanguinary than sanguine. The 99 reporting institutions had lost a total of 459 staff positions – which works out to an average of about 5.5 jobs per institution among those for which losses were reported and an average of 4.7 jobs per institution among all respondents including those reporting no losses.

The heaviest losses, in general, were in the education, curatorial, and administrative areas, while sales shop personnel were the least affected. Unfortunately, this survey data provides no way of knowing how broad a range of positions may have been reported as "administrative." I suspect, however, that many "administrative" losses involved clerical or other general support personnel whom I had not specifically categorized in the survey. Mea culpa!

The full breakdown of staff losses by category was as follows:

- Administrative – 64% of all respondents
- Education – 61%
- Curatorial – 58%
- Development – 45%
- Maintenance – 43%
- Sales Shop – 32%

Losses in a wide range of "other" staff functions were reported by 51% of respondents. These included the functions or positions of: archivist, librarian, marketing, volunteer coordinator, gardener, visitor services, public relations, exhibits (including designers, preparators, and technicians), conservator, registrar, publications, business/office personnel, restoration carpenter, facilities manager, restaurant staff, and "operations". The greatest number of layoffs specifically identified in the "other" category involved marketing personnel and individuals directly involved with provision of visitor services.

The survey did not ask specifically about the percentage of total staff affected by layoffs (mea culpa, once again), but that information was volunteered in several instances and averaged around 25%. It is no coincidence, I suspect, that 25-30% is an approximation that has been reported for the loss in value of conservative investments, such as institutional endowments, in the final months of 2008, with no end yet in sight.

Very obviously, even on the basis of this rather superficial sampling, there are museums and related institutions of every type and size currently shedding staff in response and in proportion to the "perfect storm" of fiscal adversity that has impacted even the most responsibly managed organizations like a tsunami of red ink.

It might be argued that the disappearance of a few hundred jobs, as documented by this "snapshot" survey, is an insignificant droplet in the ocean of recession-driven unemployment currently being reported across the United States and around the world. Even within the far more limited universe of museums, it's a small figure.

On the other hand, if the situation in the 99 reported institutions is at all representative of the museum community at large, then one might realistically extrapolate a nationwide loss amounting to tens of thousands of museum positions, which would be pretty frightening. Moreover, that number would represent only a retrospective count of losses which have already been announced. One can project a variety of scenarios, none of them very encouraging, about what may yet be in store as institutions batten down the budgetary hatches and prepare for a stormy year or years ahead. Clearly, it's going to be a rough ride for institutions and their employees alike.

Tina Nolan, as the Guest Editor of this issue of the *Journal of Museum Education*, has asked me to summarize this survey data and to offer a bit of commentary and/or speculation as to its significance with specific reference to museum education, which I'll attempt to do. I must admit at the outset, however, that my own museum background (over the past 40 plus years) has been primarily in the registrarial/curatorial area, as an institutional staff member, as a consultant/contractor, and as an institutional trustee who has had to deal with nitty-gritty budgeting challenges which have sometimes required the layoffs of highly valued staff. I have, however, often been involved in the planning, conduct, and evaluation of education programs and, in fact, began my long association with museums as a graduate student in geology doing school programs at the Boston Children's Museum.

I was struck by the fact that education staff (with 90 reported layoffs, one vacant position "frozen," and losses reported by more than 60% of respondents) seemed to have taken a disproportionately heavy hit from the budgetary hammers, and I could not help but wonder why this would be. For purposes of comparison, it is worth noting that museum sales shop staff suffered losses at only 32% of the reporting institutions – for a total of just 16 layoffs.

That comparison, I would suggest, should be a topic for serious discussion among museum educators and between educators and the administrators and/or governing bodies of the institutions that they serve. What does it say about the role of educators, and about institutional missions and priorities, if educators are perceived (as the survey seems to suggest) as being much more expendable than sales shop personnel?

I am inclined to believe (and this is mere speculation, not supported by any specific survey data) that museum educators are widely perceived by administrators and trustees alike as being primarily if not exclusively associated with programs for visiting school groups. If that perception is accepted (whether or not it is valid), then it is not irrational to conclude that declining school visitation numbers and revenues justify, or even demand, a proportionate reduction in education staff.

This makes me wonder how well museum educators have educated their institutions as to the multiple other ways and programs in which their particular skills and training can and should play useful roles – generating "value" not only in terms of furthering an institution's visionary mission but also by contributing to the various revenue streams needed to sustain the institution's programs and its very existence.

How many institutions regularly, effectively, and affectively use educators in developing, implementing, and evaluating their exhibits, their special events, their publications, their planned giving and other development initiatives, their assessment and planning of collections, and yes, even the selection and display of goods for their sales shops? I haven't a clue, but there is a fit topic for another survey, for conversations among educators, and for some conference sessions at the state, regional, and national level.

Having once been in the position of being involuntarily and unexpectedly laid off by a museum, I can readily empathize with those currently facing the reality or even the possibility of such a circumstance. It is a stressful and discouraging situation at best, particularly for those who may find themselves forced into a different and probably less gratifying line of work just to make ends meet.

I am equally concerned about the institutions and colleagues that laid-off educators leave behind. Ironically, these may turn out to be the ones most seriously impacted by the departure of laid-off staff. If layoffs have targeted the most senior personnel, whose salaries might offer the greatest cost-cutting potential, then the institution and its more junior staff members will be deprived of experience and leadership. If layoffs have targeted more junior staff members as expendables, then the remaining leaders will be deprived of the "followership" needed to motivate and reward their best efforts and to assure the continuity of institutional programs, values, and mission.

Both the short and long-term impacts of staff reductions are difficult to assess, and any detailed analysis is far beyond the scope of my very modest survey. In some cases, no doubt, functional gaps created by layoffs or by the freezing of vacant positions will be addressed by attempting to stretch re-maining staff time and effort to fill those voids, but it is unlikely that full-time responsibilities (particularly those involving specialized skills and training) can be adequately "covered" by personnel whose training, expe-rience, and primary responsibilities lie in other areas.

Staff capabilities and energies, like pizza dough, can be stretched only so far before gaping holes appear. In some cases, those holes will appear randomly and unpredictably as everyone tries his/her best to keep his/her institution functioning with downsized resources. In other cases, conscious decisions will be made to selectively abandon certain programs and functions or to "mothball" them until fiscal resources are sufficient to support their reactivation. In either case, a great deal of experience, skill, practical know-how, and institutional memory will have been lost to individual institutions and to the museum community, perhaps irretrievably, as laid-off staff seek and find employment elsewhere.

Perhaps the most optimistic short-term hope for institutions and per-sonnel alike is that staffing cutbacks will lead to a more realistic assessment of what are or are not "core" and "sustainable" functions, and that there may be a greater motivation for institutions to share resources (including per-sonnel) whose availability is "essential," but which may not be required on an exclusive and full-time basis. The potentials for collaborative exhibitions and programs, for sharing of collection storage facilities, for utilization of "on call" or "circuit-riding" registrars/curators/conservators/designers, etc., may all be worthy of exploration.

To be sure, such initiatives would not provide for the restoration of all laid-off staff. In fact, they might assure that some vacated positions would never be re-filled on a full-time basis even if revenues were to return to pre-recession levels — but they could provide for re-employment, or continued employment, of many who would otherwise be out of work and whose skills and experience might otherwise be permanently lost to the museum community.

I plan to keep the current survey active so long as responses continue to trickle in, and will periodically report any changes in the accumulated data that seem significant. I must say, however, that the general pattern of survey responses has been apparent, and consistent, ever since the first responses were recorded. It seems unlikely that the picture will change significantly unless there is a corresponding change, for better or for worse, in the overall economy.

The URL address for the "Museum Staff Recessionary Cutbacks" survey is: http://www.surveymonkey.com/s.aspx?sm=YUvEbEXmMu216_2b9eFbEJ_2bQ_3d_3d

Ron Kley is a partner in the consulting/contracting firm of Museum Research Associates, headquartered in Hallowell, Maine. He has worked in and for museums since the 1960s, primarily in the collection management field, but with numerous involvements in museum and "living history" educational programs.

Welcome, Mr. Director, and Good Luck!

Rafael Rosa

Abstract Museum education leaders often find themselves thrust into greater responsibility without an opportunity to prepare themselves for the challenges ahead. In this article, I discuss my own struggles transitioning from manager of a specific program area to oversight of an entire education department. This transition happened unexpectedly, and the opportunity for promotion arose faster than I had planned for. I recount the difficulty learning the content and pedagogy associated with programs with which I was not familiar, concerns I had advocating for these program areas to senior management and external partners, my feeling of isolation given I had no peers at the institution with the same responsibilities as myself, and my struggle to balance the needs of the institution as a whole with those of my department—especially when they seemed at odds. I recount the efforts I have made to grow into the position, my successes and continuing challenges, and the need for opportunities to more formally prepare museum education personnel for growing responsibility as they progress in their careers.

After 16 years in the field of museum education, I abruptly found myself in charge of a museum education department. With a staff of over 20 people working together on dozens of programs both at the museum and in the community it was quite a change from my previous level of responsibility. I was asked to take the role of Acting Director after the previous department head unexpectedly left to pursue other opportunities. While I knew that I would like to eventually advance in my career, I was not prepared for the opportunity when it arose. Given my passion for the institution and my enthusiasm for the role, I was officially promoted to Director of Education after only a few short months. Although "Acting" was no longer part of the title, it often felt that acting was what I was doing as each day presented new

Journal of Museum Education, Volume 34, Number 2, Summer 2009, pp. 129-138.

challenges and responsibilities that I had not considered when I so whole-heartedly accepted the promotion. I realized that 16 years in the field of museum education, holding titles from Educator to Manager, had not prepared me as I thought it would for the level at which I now found myself. In the three years since, I have come to discover that my situation was not an isolated one, and that many museum education leaders regardless of title (Manager, Director, Vice-President, etc.) have faced similar and sometimes more difficult transitions to a greater leadership role in their institution. Why have so many of us felt unprepared to make the transition to greater leadership? I will address this question from the perspective of my experiences and discuss some of the efforts I have made to improve my own effectiveness as a museum educational leader.

As with many people in the museum education field, the journey to my current role was circuitous. Twenty years ago, after completing an engineering degree, I realized that what I had enjoyed the most about my educational career was not the specific content I had studied, but the *process* of learning and the opportunities I had had to teach content to others. Thinking that engineering might limit my chances to pursue teaching and learning to the extent that I would like, I began to seek jobs that would allow me to share my love of learning and teaching with others. This eventually led to a part-time job as a guide at a major science museum through which my interest in education grew. Because of my science background and public speaking skills, I began to work with the education department to develop and implement programs for the general public and discovered that not only did I enjoy this work, but I seemed to be fairly good at it as well. My managers provided me more opportunities to develop programming and hone my presentation skills. After a few years, I used the skills I had gained to move to a Museum Outreach Educator position at the Chicago Academy of Sciences (and its Peggy Notebaert Nature Museum, which opened a few years later). This began my 17 year career at that institution, and it is where I am today.

When I transitioned to Director of Education, I envisioned a role that would be similar to that of Education Manager but with responsibility for even more programs and a freer hand in guiding the direction of our educational initiatives. While true to some extent, the position encompassed much, much more. For now, let us begin with the challenge I had expected, that of overseeing more programs.

Our education department, like most (large or small) includes programming for a wide range of audiences. We provide free daily programming

Teachers participating in ongoing professional development workshops at the Chicago Academy of Sciences and its Peggy Notebaert Nature Museum. *Courtesy of the Peggy Notebaert Nature Museum.*

for the general public, workshops for teachers and their students, lectures and workshops for adult audiences, classes for early childhood education providers, programs for families, activities for seniors, and much more. Increasingly, our staff is also providing activities at schools and community organizations as we try to expand our programming to a wider and more diverse audience. For most of my museum career I focused on student and teacher programs — the most "formal" of our audiences.

I had gradually come to learn the skills necessary to be effective as an educator and leader within this area of programming. Over the years I had been able to study and understand the science curricular goals and objectives teachers and students need to address, learn, and apply the best pedagogical approaches to classroom instruction, observe my colleagues as they taught in these settings, and develop relationships with teachers and administrators necessary to allow for true collaboration to improve science learning. Unfortunately, time was not available to give the same attention to the new programming for which I was now responsible. As I began to learn more about the other programs, I became increasingly aware of the limits of my knowledge in interpretation, in working with teen audiences, in early childhood education, etc. As leader of the entire department, I now had to provide guidance for programs that required many different skill sets to accomplish. I had to oversee staff that in some areas knew much more than myself about the pedagogy and content of the programs they were presenting. Given that my formal training was in science content and not educational pedagogy, this has actually been a challenge at all levels of my professional development.

Of greatest concern to me was my difficulty in advocating for the importance of the educational component of our public programming — an area in which I had not worked for over ten years at that point. I found it difficult to quickly articulate a clear vision for this area, which made it hard for me to defend my position that certain suggestions for programming from senior management and elsewhere did not fit with a coherent vision for educational programming in this area. Even after three years, I still struggle with my imbalance of knowledge in our educational programming areas.

Heading the Education Department also made me a member of the museum's senior management team — responsible for working together to chart the direction of the institution as a whole. As a manager, I was an advocate for my programs and staff knowing that when decisions were made that were not optimal for my specific programs, they were usually done to support the overall mission of the education department or the institution. However, I now had to make those decisions myself or sometimes had to support decisions that were viewed as best for the institution even when they had negative impacts on the Education Department. Supporting a "broader vision" proved to be difficult as I did not feel ready to make these hard decisions. This was especially true since I began my tenure just as we were starting a strategic planning process. It proved difficult to provide vision that properly incorporated all aspects of our programming when I was only beginning to understand a large part of it.

My new position also required quickly learning a wide array of other skills necessary to effectively operate at this level. These included an increased and more public role as a representative of the museum to our various constituencies, management of a much larger budget and understanding of the interaction between my own budget and that of the other departments, greater involvement in grant prospecting and writing, and more involvement in our program marketing. Additionally, I oversaw our entire volunteer program. I also found myself interacting with a new level of leaders both within and outside the museum. I now had direct contact with the museum's Board of Trustees and represented the museum on a variety of outside committees. Even given over a decade of experience at the Academy of Sciences, the learning curve was intimidating.

As a manager, I had peers within the education department whom I could speak to about issues and ask them to work through them with me. I also had my own supervisor who understood my programs and team. Now, as department head, I felt very alone. I no longer had peers in education and my colleagues on the senior management team were not educators. To add to the challenges, as a long term employee of the Academy and Nature Museum, several of the people that I now supervised had been my peers and friends—how was I to manage them?

So, given the challenges of leadership I've outlined and the fact that I have remained in the position for almost three years, how did I overcome these barriers? The short answer is that I have not entirely. I have learned a significant amount and have grown as a leader but still have a way to go. I have taken a variety of actions to improve my ability to lead my large and wide-ranging department which I can share.

Whether you are leading your department or serve in another capacity, for most of us, you are in all likelihood the only person at the institution filling the role that you do. This can lead to the feeling that you are on your own, as I sometimes felt. However, you are not really alone. Whether through conference networking, professional organizations, email listservs, etc., it is vital to contact people in similar positions at other institutions. I have been especially lucky in Chicago to have a very active organization of Education Directors that meet on a bi-monthly basis. Through our formal meetings and the informal gatherings that sometimes arise from them, we have been able to openly discuss many of the issues I have mentioned and the solutions we have reached. Sometimes the ideas offered are helpful and sometimes not, but having a network of peers that can be called upon for advice and suggestions is invaluable. For those of you for whom this type of direct contact may be difficult to achieve, the growth in social networking via the internet offers options that weren't available even a few years ago. Seek out the professional organizations and websites that most reflect the work you are doing and make contact.

While no one else at your institution may have the same educational responsibilities as yourself, there may be other staff members that can support your professional growth in areas for which you bear responsibility. For me, developing a close working relationship with our CFO and staff in the Marketing and Development Department has been critical. Understanding the broader fiscal, marketing, and grant prospecting strategies of the institution has given me a better appreciation for the needs of the institution as a whole, while at the same time helping me to better articulate the needs of my own department within the context of these institutional goals. Initially, I struggled to make these connections, being concerned that questions I might ask would show my own lack of knowledge in areas that I felt I should understand better. It is one of the oldest educational adages that there are no stupid questions—take it to heart. Overcoming my initial trepidation has strengthened my ability to make informed decisions and lead my department. Better understanding our finances, grant, and marketing strategies also make it easier for me to explain to my own staff how and why certain institutional decisions are made.

One unanticipated outcome of the current economic crisis is that it has required the senior management team to work more closely together to monitor our financial health and assure that we continue to fully support the institution's mission. It has opened a greater window into our financial

Growth and Leadership without Advancement, A Case Study

In my efforts to better understand the challenges faced by myself and others in our field, I have spoken to museum education professionals who are at different points in their careers and with different levels of responsibility. One concern expressed often is how to keep the best of our staff engaged given the limited number of advancement opportunities available within the museum education field. As staff gain experience, how do we recognize it, provide a greater voice for them in decision-making, and create other opportunities for their professional growth? Of special interest to me have been those who are not seeking advancement but crave the opportunity to grow within the positions they hold.

One such person I spoke with has served in her current role for over ten years and is considering the question of where to go now. She continues to enjoy her job as a coordinator and does not necessarily see herself moving on to a level that would take her further away from the responsibilities she currently has. She enjoys working closely with the public and volunteers and does not want to move to a position that would reduce her interaction with them. However, given the length of her experience she has, she feels frustrated in her ability to have her voice heard.

A structural change several years ago shifted her from one department to another. Her responsibilities did not change, but moving her position out of the education department did seem to change the way in which her role was perceived and has, over time, led to a loss of understanding as to how much practical experience she has with informal education. She feels that she has a significant amount of experience to offer to both education and exhibits staff given her direct contact with the public and the volunteers restructure that has greatly improved my understanding of how we operate and forged much stronger bonds among team members. It is unfortunate that external factors were required to accomplish this but it has strengthened my own leadership abilities; in the future, regardless of where I find myself, I will make sure to seek this sort of collaboration with my peers early on.

To improve the understanding of my department and its programs by other departments, I have tried to increase the interactions between my team members, other staff, and the senior management team. This means that when I am working on a new grant with Development I make sure that the staff that have the most knowledge of the program area are involved; that Marketing works directly with the staff for which material is being developed; and I more closely involve my team in budgetary and other decisions. Initially I made the mistake of "shielding" them from much of this so as to not unduly increase their workload. This resulted in my having to make some decisions without all the knowledge I should have had and also to a feeling by many staff of not being fully informed as to why decisions were made.

sponsible for interpretation of the exhibits to the public. But, how does that knowledge get shared if her role is seen primarily as that of recruiting and training volunteers only?

Addressing an issue such as this requires a proactive stance by the individual. If your input is not being sought, look for opportunities where it can be easily offered. Make sure that staff within your own and other departments are aware of your skills and experience. Be cognizant of the way in which information is best communicated to your colleagues as the proper approach will improve the possibility that your knowledge will be considered in the future. Additionally, seek opportunities to showcase your knowledge via conference presentations, workshops for peers at other organizations, and publication of what you have learned in print journals and online. Ultimately, raise your profile to make colleagues more aware of your experience and expertise.

While not the case with the person above, remaining in one position for a long period of time at one institution can mean changes in supervision either as other staff leave or departments are reorganized. With these changes comes a loss of direct understanding of the depth of knowledge of that staff member and potential undervaluing of her contributions given that she had not advanced within the organization or sought opportunities elsewhere. A person in this situation has the same challenges as above with the added issue of having to work with someone possibly new to his/her own role. Again, it is important that you clearly explain your role and potential for more. Be confident in what you know and can do.

Ultimately the decision as to whether you can achieve your professional goals in your current position and organization is yours. Assess the possibilities and make the decision that will give you the greatest satisfaction in the long term.

More openness and involvement with decision-making has allowed for more transparency and hopefully professional growth for the staff. As an education department, we are currently working through the best way to increase the opportunities for all levels of staff to contribute and to be made aware of and involved in important decisions that I and the rest of the senior management team need to make.

At my level of responsibility, it was also important to develop a strong relationship with members of the Board of Trustees. It was important for me to identify those individuals that had the greatest interest in and passion for our education programs, and to work closely with them. I needed their support to find the best ways to inform and educate the rest of the Board about the importance of what we want to accomplish and the resources necessary to do the work. It was heartening for me to realize that our Board members are extremely passionate about the institution and its mission. However, as volunteers, they have a limited amount of time to devote to the organization. Learning how to clearly and succinctly convey information about my department to them was critical. I have been lucky to have had strong support from the Board.

Knowing the limits of my knowledge in certain areas of the department, it has been very important for me to surround myself with staff who can fill my knowledge gaps and who I can trust to develop and implement programs that fulfill our museum's mission. While I have a depth of knowledge in certain content areas, I cannot be expected to be the expert in every possible educational and content area for which I have responsibility. I must rely on the expertise of my team to support the work we are accomplishing. However, it is important to understand the goals and objectives of each programming area, to clearly articulate them to my team and other departments and to trust that the team I have in place can accomplish them.

Rest assured that while I have found the challenges of being a department leader daunting, in general I have enjoyed the transition. It did take some time for that feeling to develop as initially I felt quite overwhelmed. Learning most of what I needed to "on the job" was not ideal but ultimately succeeded to a large degree. I hope that more formal programs related specifically to museum educational leadership are developed that can standardize to some extent the training process for future leaders and ease the transitions we face. Until that occurs, it is upon us to seek out the support and knowledge we need to succeed as we progress in our careers.

Rafael Rosa is the Vice President of Education, Chicago Academy of Sciences and its Peggy Notebaert Nature Museum. Rosa was appointed Director of Education in 2006. He has been part of the Institution's education team for over 16 years and has served in a variety of roles. He has given presentations at numerous conferences focused on environmental, technology, and science education. He currently serves as Chair of the Museums in the Park Education Committee and was recently promoted to Vice President of Education.

A Conversation about
Educational Leadership in Museums

Leslie Bedford

Abstract On February 26, 2009 the *Journal of Museum Education* hosted a telephone conversation among five senior museum educators. Leslie Bedford, Director of the Leadership in Museum Education Program at Bank Street College, facilitated the discussion with Mary Ellen Munley, Randy Roberts, Elsa Bailey, and Brigid Globensky. They shared their thinking on the theory and practice of educational leadership today. The conversation was recorded and will be available as a podcast.

The *Journal of Museum Education* recently convened a conversation about museum educational leadership. Building on ideas raised in earlier issues, the goal was to address museum educational leadership — in theory and in practice — in light of new trends in our field. As director of a graduate program in museum educational leader and long-time museum professional, I chaired the hour and one half conversation with four outstanding educational leaders: Mary Ellen Munley, independent consultant and former head of education at the Field Museum and the New York State Museum; Randy Roberts, consultant, Association Manager for the Visitor Studies Association and doctoral student in leadership and change; Elsa Bailey, currently in independent evaluation practice and former Director of Teacher Education at the Miami Museum of Science and Ph.D. in Educational Studies with a domain of museum-school partnerships; and Brigid Globensky, Director of Education at the Milwaukee Public Museum with a background in community organizing and a doctorate in American Studies. Because the conversation is will be available as a podcast at the Museum Education Roundtable's web site this short paper does not cover all the details of our rich discussion but focuses on three subtopics: some big ideas or theories that we found

    139

most applicable today, the specific skills and habits of mind we thought educational leaders needed, and finally thoughts on how one might go about learning to be a (better) leader.

THE BIG IDEA

Among the five of us on the phone, three hold Ph.D.s, one is in process, and the fifth did all but her dissertation. If nothing else, this was a well-read group. But it was not typical of museum educators (or educational leaders) whom as Bailey describes in her research do not usually have graduate degrees in the field but come from highly diverse backgrounds and learn on the job.[1] While this diversity is a strength in many if not all ways, the paucity of big ideas often animating the practice is lamentable. As Roberts pointed out, the kinds of questions educators typically pose to panelists at conference sessions tend to focus on logistics; the immediate pressure of the "how to" seems to overwhelm the attention to "why."

In my opinion there is nothing more useful than a good theory; it helps you shape your practice intentionally, clarify goals, provide benchmarks for success, and convince others you know what you are doing. For instance, in my own case, reading George Hein's *Learning in the Museum* finally brought 20 years of work as an educator in classrooms and then museums into focus.

Munley and Roberts have been working for four years with the ideas of Mark Moore and Mark Weinberg, professors at Harvard University and Ohio University, respectively, who teach and write about public value.[2] They think that Moore's theory of maximizing public value can and should be applied to museum work. Munley in particular would say that for decades museum education has focused on personal transformation, on teaching particular audiences, and providing a bridge between museum collections and the individual learner. A grounding in scholars like Dewey or Vygotsky gives the educator the theory for facilitating this experience. But, she would argue, museums are not simply about personal growth; they are also about social change. They need to consider, practice, and make visible their value to the public in ways that expand beyond the walls of the museum and then loop back to change the institution itself. Using Moore's work as a guide, it is the alignment of mission and operational capacity with the needs of audiences and communities that is at the heart of maximizing public value.

One example of this kind of educational work is the long-term initiative at the United States Holocaust Memorial Museum called "Bringing the

Lessons Home".[3] This program involves training Washington, D.C. teens in the lessons and history of the Holocaust and then empowering them to teach on the floor. Inspired by what they have learned, these young people invariably want to act on their new knowledge; they want to move beyond their own transformation, and for that they need the museum's help. Working off of the ideas of Moore and the museum's own core, if previously not fully articulated values, Munley and Roberts helped the museum envision new roles for itself as a model of civic engagement and a convener and resource for active citizens. In other words, the museum is moving beyond the conventional program for teens, familiar to virtually every institution, into the arena of youth and community development.

Bailey likened this project to the Dewitt Wallace-Reader's Digest Fund (now the Wallace Foundation) funded initiative *Youth*ALIVE! which ran from 1990 to 1999. *Youth*ALIVE! programs were conducted in more than 70 science centers/museums and children's museums across the country. In many cases, there was evidence that this program had multiple effects. Not only were there positive impacts on the participating youth, but also this work with local adolescents from diverse groups appeared to have brought about changes in the involved staff, their institutions, and their relationships with their community-based organizations. In other words, *Youth*ALIVE! strongly influenced the culture of the participating museums, and in some cases, their public face.[4]

Globensky described one program at the Milwaukee Art Museum, which illustrates how a museum's commitment to its community can create a ripple effect. The museum hosts a program for a diverse group of young people who work together for a year on a social issue of their own choosing; they do research outside the museum and into artists who have explored social issues. As a group they design a mural, which becomes a "wrap-around" for Milwaukee buses for one year. The impact expands through what she calls "teach to learn"; the teens who work together on art and social issues then introduce students from a local Community Learning Center to the museum and the teens' project. The real change for the museum happens in the second year of the internship when ten teens work at the museum for a year working on-line, giving gallery talks, and developing a public program for teens. As Globensky explained, "How they look at and think about the Museum changes us. They have also changed how we think of the Internet. Last year one of our teen interns won an award for the top ten teen web sites in the country."

A second set of ideas dealt with leadership, the topic of numerous trade books. Phrases like "collaborative leadership" or "distributive leadership" embody challenges to the discredited but still omnipresent "heroic" leadership in many institutions. Roberts mentioned a leadership approach that is particularly applicable in today's dynamic environment: adaptive leadership.[5] Adaptive leaders acknowledge and work with the multiple, often competing, values found within and outside the institution. They provide a space where distress is kept at a "tolerable level," work focuses on the important rather than the urgent, and those most affected by the outcome are given a voice. The leader's role is to mobilize rather than enforce a personal vision. The adaptive leader is not bogged down in old tricks or tired technical solutions but strives to understand what the real current issues are.[6]

An example of adaptive leadership at work came from Bailey's experience at the Museum Advocacy Days on Capitol Hill. She felt that the American Association of Museums (AAM) had successfully convened a group of museum professionals, educated them to the realities of how museums are perceived outside the field, and then given them training that presented new skills for building a convincing case and communicating this case to their elected representatives and other policy makers and drivers.

SKILLS FOR PRACTITIONERS AND HOW TO GET THEM

The conversation about leadership helped the group members identify what they think are the skills today's museum educational leaders need to cultivate. Munley believes that educators are in the position—they have the opportunity—to help their institutions think more boldly. Or as I often say to students joining the Bank Street Museum Leadership Program, educators have many of the personal qualities and habits of mind of effective leadership; they are idealistic and empathetic, communicative, other-directed people with great passion for their work. In fact, a good leader at whatever level is also an educator. But these are really attributes. What are the skills the work requires and where are they to be found?

The group agreed that too often educators (and others as well, of course) do not look outside their own role or department. They may not understand how their work meshes with that of the institution as a whole. Uninformed about the big picture, they cannot think strategically or argue convincingly for an idea or a program.

Thinking strategically may be the most important task to master. It requires not only knowing how your institution sits within its community, and

The Bank Street Museum Leadership Program Class of 2007 visits Philip Johnson's Glass House during its June Institute.

the field as a whole, but what will help move it along its chosen path to greater success. Bailey spoke of leaving her institution to go to graduate school, reading in the field of organizational development and communities of practice,[7] and then going back to share her insights with her former director in how she had come to realize how important it was for mid-level people to understand how their work and departments fit within the bigger institutional mission; she became encouraged to put more emphasis on "the big picture" when working with staff.

A second set of skills had to do with forging internal as well as external alliances. Lacking an understanding of the strategic vision, educators and education departments can create barriers between themselves and others. Marketing or curatorial or development become the enemy to the education department's self-anointed role as "good guys." A failure to build internal alliances may work well enough during good times but our tumbling economy requires a savvier grasp of the institution as a whole and the value of working together. Educators know about building partnerships; they need to understand these are internal as well as external.

Channeling the thinking of many of my students, I asked the group how one could both think strategically and help add public value to the museum when you are not the boss. There were several suggestions. One was to "go rogue"—operate under the radar or revert to guerilla tactics. Sometimes this works well, especially if it yields demonstrable evidence of positive change; as Bailey said, it's good to have real world examples to support your argument. An alternative was Globensky's suggestion that staff need to understand

things from the boss' position and respond to his strengths rather than em-
phasizing differences. Those of us who attended the Museum Management
Institute could testify to the value of negotiation, of reframing difficult
problems, and the other approaches described in books like *Getting to Yes*.[8] In
any case, the experienced educator's ability to put herself in someone else's
shoes is a useful leadership skill as well.

So where are educators to get these—and many other—skills? Few
museums appear to invest in significant or continuous professional development. One exception is the Boston Children's Museum, which recently

Transforming Education Theory into Practice

I knew it would be challenging to attend the Leadership in Museum Education program at Bank Street College while working full time at The Corning Museum of Glass, not to mention that I had one child in third grade and another not yet in kindergarten. I had meant to wait at least until my son started school, but Leslie Bedford, Director of the program, convinced me that I needed to start the coming year. The program alternates between a year focused on education and a year focused on management. The education year was coming next, and I was very interested in the education year. Leslie always makes a very compelling argument, so I listened and started the program right away.

Having a supportive family really helped me manage the requirements of the program and having a supportive employer allowed me to thrive during my Bank Street period. I was constantly bringing back new ideas and discussing them with my colleagues. I began to view the Corning Museum with a global vision rather than viewing it from my areas of direct responsibility.

One of the great things about the program was being exposed to so many different professionals from other museums;

the students all worked for museums and the presenters worked with or for yet other museums. In this program, classes meet on weekends once a month for two years, and then there is a one week long session each June. The third year consists of independent thesis work. Each weekend was really a think tank full of ideas.

I brought back new ways to transform education theory into practice in our programs. Because of Bank Street, my Director let me run with new programs that incorporated Bank Street ideas. Two programs that are now part of our programming and have become parts of our museum's culture came directly from this new thinking. Our *Families Explore* series is a program that investigates the cultures represented in our collection through music, dance, crafts, food, and other activities. It involves participation by members of some of the areas different national and ethnic communities. The *Explainer* program teaches high school students about the art, history, and science of glass. It also builds self-confidence and teaches presentation skills. After successfully completing the training program, the students are eligible for peak-season employment in our galleries, where they engage visitors in conver-

launched its BCM Institute, a series of in-house sessions for mid-career program staff.[9] While there are a handful of graduate programs that focus on or include leadership training in the curriculum, most practitioners depend on conferences and other *ad hoc* methods for keeping abreast of new ideas. Such ventures are expensive, and these days museums are even less likely to subsidize staff participation. The answer may ultimately lie in on-line technologies such as the webinars and blogs that professional organizations including AAM and the Center for the Future of Museums have launched.

But there are other things one can do. Early in her career Munley learned

sation about different aspects of glass and glassmaking during the busy summer months. Never before had we done anything in our galleries except display objects and give basic docent-led tours.

Bank Street also got me thinking about our exhibitions. At first I was invited to sit in on exhibition planning meetings, and for many months I listened and absorbed. Full of enthusiasm from what I'd been learning, I began to test ideas about ways we could add to the learning components for the general audience of our exhibitions. We are now incorporating various learning components—audio, video, text geared toward a family audience, and interactive areas—into our exhibitions.

Although I had been involved in many aspects of the day-to-day leadership of the museum, my exposure at Bank Street to management issues gave me a broad view of areas that I had not thought much about, like governance and boards. Although our mission is about collecting and educating, members of our leadership team need to understand the intricacies of how the board works.

Almost all the members of my class came from education departments at various museums. At Corning, the education department's mission is closely aligned with the mission of the museum as

a whole; however, the leadership of a museum needs a broader view, a view of the institution as a whole. Leadership needs to have an understanding of the entire institution and not just a single part of it. The experience at Bank Street informed that view for me. It strengthened my views of how best to lead a museum in incorporating this global view: thinking about the objects, the people using the museum, and the people supporting the museum. I went to Bank Street to learn about education in a museum but I came away with a much broader view of how museums can best be a vibrant part of their communities.

Amy Schwartz, Director of Development, Education & The Studio, Corning Museum of Glass. In 1995, Amy Schwartz joined The Corning Museum of Glass to create an artistic and educational glassworking facility called The Studio. In 2002, Ms. Schwartz took on the additional responsibility of overseeing Education Programs for the entire Museum. In 2007, she added development director to her responsibilities. Ms. Schwartz maintains her own glassblowing practice, designing and making functional and decorative objects. In 2007, Ms. Schwartz received a Master of Science Degree in Leadership in Museum Education from the Bank Street College of Education. She holds a Bachelors Degree from the State University of New York at Binghamton.

the value of volunteering; for instance, serving on a professional committee became her introduction to another area of the field. When I first moved to New York from Boston I convened a group of museum people for monthly evening get-togethers; while the impetus was the desire for professional friends, the result was an entire education. Gather up your staff and go on a road trip or invite someone whose ideas you admire to come by and talk with staff over lunch. And keep reading. In other words, you need to count on yourself—in addition to your institution—to teach you what you want and need to learn. As we like to say at Bank Street, leadership begins at your own desk.

Notes

1. Elsa B. Bailey, "How Museum Educators Build and Carry Out Their Profession: An Examination of Situated Learning within Practice" (Ph.D. Diss., Lesley University, 2003).
2. Mark H. Moore, *Creating Public Value: Strategic Management in Government* (Cambridge, MA: Harvard University Press, 1995).
3. Begun in 1994, just one year after the United States Holocaust Memorial and Museum (USHMM) opened, *Bringing the Lessons Home* is a program that provides students from the Washington, DC area high schools with a learning opportunity focused on connecting current social issues with the history and lesson of the Holocaust. An evaluation of the program completed in 2008 is available from the Education Department of the USHMM up on request.
4. For further discussion of the impact of *Youth*ALIVE! see http://www.astc.org/pubs/dimensions/2000/nov-dec/afterschool.htm). According to the PI on the initiative, as recently as six months ago, ten of these original programs had managed to find funding past the Wallace grants and were still going strong. For further information please write Elsa Bailey directly at ebbailey@earthlink.net.
5. Ronald A. Heifetz, *Leadership Without Easy Answers* (Cambridge, MA: Harvard University Press, 1994).
6. For a convincing discussion of how organizations frequently respond to major changes in their environment by trying to improve outmoded strategies rather than embrace new solutions, see Jay Rounds, "The Best of Practices, The Worst of Times," in *Are We There Yet? Conversations about Best Practices in Science Exhibition Development* (San Francisco: Exploratorium, 2004), 5-10.
7. There are a number of excellent sources for readers interested in organizational change, leadership and situated learning. In addition to those mentioned earlier, we would recommend the following: Lee G. Bolman and Terrence E. Deal, *Reframing Organizations: Artistry, Choice and Leadership* (San Francisco: Jossey-Bass, 1997); Yrjo.Engeström and David Middleton, eds., *Cognition And Communication at Work* (Cambridge, U.K.: Cambridge University Press, 1998); John P. Kotter, *Leading Change* (Cambridge, MA: Harvard Business School Press, 1996); Jean Lave and Etienne Wenger, *Situated Learning: Legitimate Peripheral Participation* (Cambridge, U.K.: Cambridge University Press, 1991); Peter M. Senge, *The Fifth Discipline* (paperback ed.) (New York: Doubleday, 1990/1994) and "The Leader's New Work: Building Learning Organizations," *Sloan Management Review*. MIT. (Fall 1990); Etienne Wenger, *Communities of Practice: Learning, Meaning, and Identity* (Cambridge, U.K.: Cambridge University Press, 1998).
8. Roger Fisher and William L. Ury, *Getting to Yes: Negotiating Agreement Without Giving In* (New York: Penguin, 1981).

9. IMLS supports professional development through initiatives like Museums for America and 21st Century Museum Professionals. The author would be interested in learning of how institutions or partnerships are providing continuous learning for staff.

Leslie Bedford (lbedford@bankstreet.edu) has been director of the Leadership in Museum Education Program at Bank Street College in New York City since 2000. She is also an independent consultant and a member of The Museum Group. She began her museum career at the Boston Children's Museum in the early 1980's as director and senior developer of its Japan Program. Dr. Bedford holds a master's degree from Harvard Graduate School of Education and a Ph.D. from Union Institute and University. Her dissertation examines exhibitions as an art form and imaginative experience.

Shared Professional Knowledge
Implications for Emerging Leaders

Lynn Uyen Tran and Heather King

Abstract   Educators make significant contributions to museums' educational agendas, yet recognition of their status in the museum field
remains minimal. Furthermore, limited research has been directed at the
nature of their practice and pedagogy. By establishing a common body
of knowledge underpinned by theory and leading to a shared framework
for practice, it is argued that emerging leaders in the field will be equipped
to know how best how to design, manage and implement initiatives that
support learning. Elsewhere, we have proposed just such a theoretically
grounded knowledge base to inform educator practice.[1] In this paper we
share exemplars from a current study in which we explore the interconnections between our proposed knowledge base and the complexity of
museum educators' work. Our findings demonstrate the need for
emerging leaders in museum education to have a deep understanding of
the knowledge that underlies their work. Without this knowledge, we
assert that emerging leaders will be ill equipped to guide their staff
towards a set of proven practices that support visitor learning. Moreover,
they will be denied a shared vocabulary with which they may defend and
further develop the educational role of their museums.

Educators have a longstanding presence in museums, and they play a significant role in an institution's educational agenda.[2] They undertake a diverse
range of tasks and have varied responsibilities. They are the human interface
between the museums' collections, the knowledge and culture that are represented, and the visiting public. They develop, coordinate, and implement
programs for schoolchildren, families, teachers, and the general public, and

thus engage with learners across a wide range of ages, interests, and abilities both on the museum floor and by way of printed and web-based materials.[3] Museum educators are involved in designing and developing exhibits and educational programs and, in some cases, conducting visitor studies on those exhibitions and programs.[4] They also create and nurture relationships with community groups in order to attract visitors and make their museums accessible, relevant, and inclusive of the people they serve.[5]

Despite these significant contributions, however, recognition of their status in the museum field remains minimal.[6] Furthermore, limited research has been directed at the nature of the pedagogical knowledge underlying the diverse range of tasks they perform.[7] We have argued elsewhere that establishing a common body of knowledge could lead to a shared framework for practice and also provide the basis for pre-service education and ongoing professional development.[8] In highlighting the theoretical underpinnings of this shared knowledge base, we argue that rightful attention will be paid to the practice of the museum educator, ensuring they receive the professional respect and recognition that they are due.

We have previously acknowledged the many issues surrounding proposals to develop education and professional development programs.[9] For example, would the requirement to undertake appropriate education based on a consensually agreed body of knowledge restrict the diversity of backgrounds and experiences that currently characterizes the museum education field? Moreover, can museums afford the higher levels of remuneration likely to be demanded by practitioners who have attained this education? We believe that if museums wish to ensure the quality of their educational provisions they need to monitor the professional preparation of their staff. Notwithstanding the future development of accredited professional programs, we argue that museums may monitor their current educational provisions by supporting those members of their staff who are emerging as leaders in the field by ensuring that they know how to use and apply a body of knowledge in order to design, manage, and implement initiatives that best support learners.[10] In addition, we note that a shared knowledge base will be essential in providing emerging leaders with a common vocabulary that they may use to defend and develop the educational role of museums in an economic climate wherein both funding and sanctions for cultural institutions are likely to be increasingly threatened.

KNOWLEDGE & COMPLEXITY OF PRACTICE

Previously, we have proposed six knowledge components to ground museum educators' practice.[11] These components are derived from theory and research on learning and teaching in science museums. We do not claim that they are exhaustive; moreover, we recognize that our examples are skewed towards science. However, we consider the components to be relevant to the whole museum sector. In brief: a knowledge of *context* requires an understanding of the ways in which the physical, social, communal, and temporal dimensions of museum environments interrelate; *choice* refers to the need to recognize the way in which learners are free to engage in topics that interest them thus nurturing their intrinsic motivation for learning; whilst a knowledge of *content* is necessary to interpret the discipline of the institution, which in general is mediated through the use of *objects*. Knowledge of *theories of learning*, meanwhile, is essential for understanding the actions of learners and for understanding and mediating the educational content of museum environments. Finally, since it is the spoken word over the written text that is favored in museums, *talk* refers to the manifold ways in which educators may communicate with learners through verbal and non-verbal actions.

In our current study, we analyze the actions of museum educators in order to explicate the intricacies of their practice and the ways in which our proposed knowledge components may support and inform their work.[12] We use video observations and stimulated recall interviews to scrutinize the actions and knowledge that underlie the practice of six educators in a science museum in the United Kingdom.[13] That is, we videotaped the educators delivering their programs, and then whilst jointly reviewing the tapes, asked them questions about particular incidents to probe the knowledge and beliefs underlying their actions. The educators concerned develop programs and directly engage with the public in three ways: gallery interpretations, auditorium shows, and classroom-based lessons.

Here we share some exemplars to describe the interconnections within our proposed knowledge components and to demonstrate the complexities of museum educators' practice. Moreover, we reflect on ways in which these interconnections can result in effective pedagogy, as suggested and supported by the research literature, and thus are necessary for an emerging leader's repertoire. We contend that all practitioners should share this knowledge, but note that leaders in the field should be particularly proficient, as it is their role to guide and inform their staff and ensure a consistently high quality of learning experiences.

Content through Objects

Objects are the "things" in museums that people go to "see"; they include, but are not limited to, artifacts, specimens, artworks, and interactive exhibits. They are what make museums different from other learning environments. These objects are the physical representations of the museum's content, and are displayed for their authenticity, immediacy, interactivity, and cultural capital. It is proposed that objects offer information unavailable in two-dimensional images; they provoke affective connections between learners and the knowledge represented; and they encourage different types of learning conversations.[14] Consequently, educators use objects as the primary vehicle for communicating content. How this occurs in practice, however, depends on who chooses the objects during an interaction—the educator or visitor.

If the educators were in the position to determine the content, they selected objects that they believed would provoke affective connections and promote conversations. For instance, in reviewing his auditorium show about bubbles, one educator noted that he wanted to explain that it was the density of gases that made bubbles sink or float. Thus he used particular objects—bubble wand, helium tank—to demonstrate a body of pre-determined content:

> [I]t works much better if you can see [helium bubbles] compared with normal [air filled] bubbles, so you can see [bubbles] going up with helium compared to going down with air....[The learners] can see the difference.

In contrast, during gallery interpretations, it was usually the learner who chose the object or appeared to be interested in an exhibit, and thus the educator was required to respond accordingly. In most instances, however, the educators focused the interactions on how to manipulate the exhibits correctly, rather than attempt to mediate the connection between the exhibits or objects to the content. Indeed, on reviewing themselves in action, some educators noted this habit in their practice, with one stating, "the explanation of what the exhibit is and how to work it tends to be the main topic that gets talked about." As a result of this self-revelation, the educator in question purposefully tried to modify her practice. In a subsequent observation and discussion she described her actions as follows:

> [The learner showed] interest in hitting the buttons, but she clearly didn't know why she was doing it. I wanted to explain what to do, but I also tried to explain a little bit about why she was doing it, and what it meant.

TALK FOR MULTI-GENERATIONAL LEARNING

Museums are social spaces that strive to invite and encourage all members of the public to visit. The groupings of visitors to museums include adult chaperones with similar-aged students in school groups, multi-generational families, individuals, and youth and adult peer groups.[15] In supporting the diverse agendas, interests, experiences, and abilities of their various learners, museum educators need to respect a group's social dynamics while also acknowledging the needs of individuals. The attempt to appeal to all learners, whilst also maintaining respect for an individual learner's personal choice, complicates an educator's practice. They must make judgments about what a group of learners are able to understand (by making assumptions about their age, background or education) and then communicate an appropriate level of content. The educators also modify their talk according to the type of interaction.

For example, in an auditorium show, one educator explained how he used questions to encourage participation and maintain motivation in an audience that ranged in age from young children to senior citizens. He noted that adults rarely answered his questions because they "think it's for the kids, they are afraid of getting it wrong, . . . or they can't be bothered." Thus he described his strategy of engaging a multi-generational audience, by dividing his content into questions for older, generally higher ability, audiences and questions for younger, generally lower ability, audiences. With reference to a section of the videotape in which he was attempting to prompt audience replies about the nature of sound, the educator explained his actions thus:

> When you're asking, "what a noise is?" . . . a kid under six . . . won't tell you it's compressions, refractions in the air. If you head up the

age scale you're more likely to get a closer answer, so I was looking for somebody older. When you're 14–16, . . . you might be quite proud that you can explain what a noise is, or what a sound is. Whereas for a six year old, I might ask questions about which sound was louder, or lower.

In this way, the educator was clearly supportive of his learners' abilities, and in looking for a willing respondent was also sensitive to the audience members' confidence to participate in front of strangers.

In gallery interpretations, however, this strategy may not be possible, as the conditions of interactions are generally different. First, the learner group is smaller and members usually know one another. Second, the group navigates the museum freely and so chooses the objects with which it wants to engage and for how long. Third, in most cases, the children within the group have a more prominent role in directing the interactions than the adults.[16]

In an attempt to convey the content, educators in our study explained that they either talked at the level of the children or had two ongoing conversations, one with the children and one with the adults. One educator articulated her strategy thus:

> . . . at an exhibit, you've got the adults thinking at one particular level and then the children at another, and sometimes even with the children you've got older kids and younger kids. Yeah it is very difficult cos where do you pitch it? I mean if you pitch it too young, no one's going to care. If you pitch it too old, the majority of them won't care. . . . If I have a big range, [I often try and pitch it for] the middle child . . . cos if you grab the kids, hopefully the parents will stay and then you can then expand on stuff if they want.

Novelty and Choice

Museums are repositories for a broad array of objects, which often create highly novel experiences. For example, museums may be the first and indeed only places where people can see the *Enola Gay* or the *Mona Lisa*, touch an African elephant or a meteorite, or engage safely with phenomena illustrating the nature of electricity. Whilst high levels of novelty have been found to stimulate curiosity and learning, they also have been shown to hinder learner engagement.[17] The freedom of choice, meanwhile, has been recognized to be important for fostering an intrinsic motivation to learn, although it is argued that guidance and structure may also be necessary in order to focus and support learning.[18] Clearly, the need to manage both the novelty and free choice afforded in museum contexts add another layer of complexity to a museum educator's practice. Again, how educators negotiate the various dilemmas depends on the type of interaction.

In organized programs, such as auditorium shows and classroom-based lessons, learners might choose to participate, but the educators nonetheless direct the flow and activities in the interactions.[19] In such instances, educators in this study used advanced organizers to address the novelty of the objects and the experience. For example, in a classroom-based lesson that included many taxidermy specimens, an educator told the students what they would see before they entered the classroom. During the stimulated recall interview, the educator explained that:

> I do that to prepare the children for what they're going to see and hear. I don't do that for most workshops. . . . I didn't used to do that . . . but from my experience I've found that the children can be a bit disturbed by seeing stuffed animals and also they can want to grab at them. And so I do that introduction so that before the children enter, they're prepared.

This educator was cognizant of the value of these objects for learning, but also understood the potential negative effects of a novel experience.

With regard to interactions in the galleries, meanwhile, learner choice was a key factor. Indeed, the educator could not make the learner engage, instead they needed to try to follow the learner's area of interest and interact accordingly. To do this, the educators noted that they tended to manage the effects of novelty and the visitors' free choice by making themselves as approachable as possible. In this way, they hoped that they would not be intimidating to a learner and thus inhibit engagement.

Learning Drives Practice

In their efforts to support engagement, educators structured their interactions with learners on the basis of their beliefs regarding the ways in which people learn. In many museums, a prevalent belief involved the notion that learners learned best by discovering concepts by themselves.[20] Indeed in our study, we found that during gallery interpretations, where educators were largely unconstrained by time or program objectives (as is the case in auditorium shows and classroom-based lessons), they appeared to be influenced by a notion of self-discovery learning. For example, one educator defended her action of refusing to answer a learner's question thus:

> . . . I just wanted to try and get him to actually sit and work out the answer for himself, cos I knew he was capable of doing it . . . rather than if I tell him, he'll forget five minutes later. But cos he's worked it out himself hopefully he'll have understood.

Benchmarking Education on the Road

Early in my tenure as Director of Education and Public Programs at the Berkshire Museum, the education staff and I organized a three-day field trip to New York City and Long Island, New York to visit a variety of museums. For me it was an important way to bond with new staff. For the team, it was a way to build a collective language with which to construct a shared vision and to improve our current practices. We called it benchmarking.[1]

To ensure that everyone shared an investment in the trip — there were to be no tag-alongs or critics — each staff member was asked to research at least two museums in the metropolitan area. After preliminary research we presented to the team "our" museums. We developed a case why we might, or might not, visit a particular museum, and, if so, what we thought the institution and its staff could offer. Once we had an idea of the museums we would like to visit and why, we determined which of their staff members with whom we would like to speak. It took some time to make contacts, talk to various staff, and to schedule a final list of visits and "in-

terviews." Finally, we drafted a list of questions for each staff member we were to meet at each museum.

During the trip we visited two children's museums, an historical society, a natural history museum, a botanical garden, and a science center. Our individual objectives varied. One team member sought ideas to inform the development of a prototype for cart and gallery discovery programs. Another desired new on-line web material for teachers, while a third wished to re-envision the docent program. Yet another would be the lead for school group visits. Therefore we met together with programming staff, education staff, front desk, and visitor services staff. Sometimes we toured as a group; other times we broke off into pairs or on our own.

We navigated museum driving directions and found (or did not find) parking options. We ate in museum cafeterias, at snack bars, or in restaurants; we used their bathrooms. We navigated way finding, floor plans, and museum maps. We read brochures, gallery guides, and family guides; listened to audio tours; par-

Whilst such practice is widespread among museum educators, we question whether it is entirely effective. Without guidance, a learner, and children in particular, may not be able to make sense of concepts and potentially leave an interaction with an incomplete or incorrect understanding of a principle.[21] We therefore assert that greater attention needs to be paid to the nature of museum educators' beliefs on, and understanding of, how people learn.

IMPLICATIONS FOR EMERGING LEADERS

In summary, the discussion above illustrates the ways in which our proposed knowledge components interconnect and inform the practices of museum

ticipated in floor demonstrations; and observed school group visits. We watched visitors come and go; we observed them in galleries or interacting with front end staff, security guards, or coat check staff.

At the end of each visit we met over lunch, a coffee break, at dinner, or in the hotel bar at night and discussed what we saw, the impressions we had. We assigned scribes and took notes. We would share what we liked best, what inspired us, what we noticed. We noted things we thought did not work, or would not work for us, and why. We compared what others were doing and how it could inform our own practice. Overall we found that not only was the trip a great way to share with peers and colleagues from other museums, to listen to their views and to hear them reflect on what they do and why, but it also opened us up to share our own opinions on our own work with each other. We even had the satisfaction to acknowledge what we did well and to congratulate ourselves.

The outcomes of our visits were sometimes unexpected; the rewards were many. It was a valuable experience to get out of the confines of the office to see how other museums and their staffs were faring.

It was a great way to find out about one another, to learn what inspired us, what energized us, and what our pet peeves were. As a team, we developed solid opinions on things to do and things to avoid. Ultimately, benchmarking was a great way to build a collective team spirit and to foster a culture of learning.

Note

1. **bench·mark▪bench·mark·ing▪ bench·marks**
   To measure according to specified standards in order to compare it with and improve one's own product.

Maria Mingalone is the Director of Interpretation at the Berkshire Museum, Massachusetts and oversees the development of exhibitions, education programs for students and teachers, as well as public programs for families and adults. Mingalone received her Masters of Science in Education from Bank Street College of Education, NY, in the Leadership in Museum Education Program. She studied art education at Pratt Institute, New York and received her BFA in studio art from S.U.N.Y. at Stony Brook.

educators. The examples emphasize the complexity of their practice. These findings underscore three reasons why emerging leaders in museum education need to have a deep understanding of the knowledge that underlies their work.

First, in understanding this shared knowledge, emerging leaders will be better able to offer their staff the intellectual and practical support they need, and in turn, build capacity within their department and museum. In addition, in reflecting on the knowledge base applied, educators and emerging leaders are able to examine, and react to, their actions, beliefs, and assumptions.[22] Second, and as a corollary of the first point, this shared knowledge will offer emerging leaders a framework to review and assess the quality of their educational provisions, and thus assist them in fostering meaningful learning experiences in museums for the visiting public.

Finally, in understanding this shared knowledge, emerging leaders will be able to contribute to and acquire the language of their field, which is vital for the professionalization process. While museum education has been professionalizing for many decades, it still lacks a common language which itself is based in a common knowledge base.[23] A shared professional discourse offers practitioners a standard means of communication to talk about their work with colleagues inside and outside of their institution.[24] Therefore, they will be able to articulate their ideas and actions coherently and consistently, which will contribute to the public recognition of the profession as legitimate.[25]

In short, we contend that knowing and consistently applying a theoretically grounded knowledge base of the field will equip emerging leaders with a framework for guiding staff and their institution in the design and implementation of quality educational provisions for learners visiting their museum.

Acknowledgments

The research study featured in this paper was made possible by a National Science Foundation grant (NSF-ESI 011978) for the *Center for Informal Learning and Schools*. The opinions, views, and conclusions expressed in this article may not reflect those of the funding agency. The authors thank the UK science museum and museum educators that gave their time and commitment to the study.

Suggested Readings

David Ebitz, "Qualifications and the Professional Preparation and Development of Art Museum Educators," *Studies in Art Education* 46, 2 (2005): 150-169. *Ebitz describes the initiatives developed by with the field of art museum education to raise the profile and ensure the caliber of art educators. He also discusses reviews of the field, which criticize staff structures and roles. This paper constitutes a valuable introduction to the issues of professionalization facing the informal learning sector.*

Lynn Uyen Tran and Heather King, "The Professionalization of Museum Educators: The Case in Science Museums," *Museum Management and Curatorship* 22, 2 (2007): 129-147. *Tran and King use the sociological discourse on professions to scrutinize the professionalization process of museum education. They argue that professionalization provides a route to greater respect and recognition for museum educators; however, this field needs to identify a theoretically derived body of knowledge to underpin the nature of its professional preparation and practice.*

Notes

1. Lynn Uyen Tran and Heather King, "The Professionalization of Museum Educators: The Case in Science Museums," *Museum Management and Curatorship* 22, no. 2 (2007): 129-47.
2. Eilean Hooper-Greenhill, *Museum and Gallery Education*, (Leicester: Leicester University Press, 1991); Joel J. Orosz, *Curators and Culture: The Museum Movement of America, 1740-1870*, (Tuscaloosa: University of Alabama Press, 1990).
3. Cornelia Brüninghaus-Knubel, "Museum Education in the Context of Museum Functions," in *Running a Museum: A Practical Handbook*, ed. Patrick J. Boylan (Paris, France: ICOM –International Council of Museums, 2006); Elsa B. Bailey, "Researching Museum Educators' Perceptions of Their Roles, Identity, and Practice," *Journal of Museum Education* 31, no. 3 (2006): 175-98.
4. Lisa C. Roberts, *From Knowledge to Narrative: Educators and the Changing Museum*, (Washington, DC: Smithsonian Institution Press, 1997); Stephen Bitgood, Beverly Serrell, and Don Thompson, "The Impact of Informal Education on Visitors to Museums," in *Informal Science Learning: What the Research Says About Television, Science Museums, and Community-Based Projects*, eds. Valerie Crane et al. (Dedham, MA: Research Communications, 1994).
5. Barbara Henry, "The Educator at the Crossroads of Institutional Change," *Journal of Museum Education* 31, no. 3 (2006): 223-32.
6. Margaret Christine Castle, "Interpreters, Docents, and Educators: Ways of Knowing, Ways of Teaching in a History Museum, an Art Gallery, and a Nature Centre," in *Curriculum, Teaching, and Learning*, vol. PhD (Toronto: University of Toronto, 2001); Elsa B. Bailey, "The Professional Relevance of Museum Educators," *Journal of Museum Education* 31, no. 3 (2006): 155-60; Leona Schauble et al., "Supporting Science Learning in Museums," in *Learning Conversations in Museums*, eds. Gaea Leinhardt, Kevin Crowley, and Karen Knutson (Mahwah, NJ: Lawrence Erlbaum Associates, 2002).
7. Lynn Uyen Tran, "Teaching Science in Museums: The Pedagogy and Goals of Museum Educators," *Science Education* 91, no. 2 (2007): 278-97; Lynn Uyen Tran, "The Work of Science Museum Educators," *Museum Management and Curatorship* 23, no. 2 (2008): 135-53.
8. Lynn Uyen Tran and Heather King, "The Professionalization of Museum Educators: The Case in Science Museums," *Museum Management and Curatorship* 22, no. 2 (2007): 129-47.
9. Ibid.
10. Emerging leaders are mid-career staff in education departments, such as coordinators, supervisors, and managers, who are interested and ready to progress on to the next level in their career trajectory.
11. Ibid.

12. Lynn Uyen Tran and Heather King, "Knowledge Informing the Actions: The Professional Practice of Science Museum Educators," (in progress).
13. John Lyle, "Stimulated Recall: A Report on Its Use in Naturalistic Research," *British Educational Research Journal* 29, no. 6 (2003): 861-78; J. Calderhead, "Stimulated Recall: A Method for Research on Teaching," *British Journal of Educational Psychology* 51, no. 2 (1981): 211-217.
14. Gaea Leinhardt and Kevin Crowley, "Objects of Learning, Objects of Talk: Changing Minds in Museums," in *Perspectives on Object-Centered Learning in Museums*, ed. Scott G. Paris (Mahwah, NJ: Lawrence Erlbaum Associates, 2002); Sharon Macdonald, "Exhibitions and Public Understanding of Science Paradox," http://www.pantaneto.co.uk/issue13/macdonald.htm (accessed 11 April, 2007); Catherine Eberbach and Kevin Crowley, "From Living to Virtual: Learning from Museum Objects," *Curator* 48, no. 3 (2005): 317-38; Jill M. Hohenstein and Lynn Uyen Tran, "The Use of Questions in Exhibit Labels to Generate Explanatory Conversation among Science Museum Visitors," *International Journal of Science Education* 29, no. 12 (2007): 1557-80.
15. Paulette M. McManus, "It's the Company You Keep: The Social Determination of Learning-Related Behavior in a Science Museum," *The International Journal of Museum Management and Curatorship* 6, no. 3 (1987): 263-270.
16. Kevin Crowley et al., "Shared Scientific Thinking in Everyday Parent-Child Activity," *Science Education* 85, no. 6 (2001): 712-732.
17. Shelley Carson, Margaret Shih, and Ellen Langer, "Sit Still and Pay Attention?," *Journal of Adult Development* 8, no. 3 (2001): 183-188; John H. Falk, W Wade Martin, and John D. Balling, "The Novel Field Trip Phenomenon: Adjustment to Novel Settings Interferes with Task Learning," *Journal of Research in Science Teaching* 15, no. 2 (1978): 127-134.
18. Mihaly Csikszentmihalyi and Kim Hermanson, "Intrinsic Motivation in Museums: What Makes Visitors Want to Learn?," *Museums News* May/June(1995): 34-37 and 59-61; Richard E. Grandy, "Constructivism and Objectivity: Disentangling Metaphysics from Pedagogy," *Science and Education* 6, no. 1-2 (1997): 43-53; Paul A. Kirschner, John Sweller, and Richard E. Clark, "Why Minimal Guidance During Instruction Does Not Work: An Analysis of the Failure of Constructivist, Discovery, Problem-Based, Experiential, and Inquiry-Based Teaching," *Educational Psychologist* 41, no. 2 (2006): 75-86.
19. Tali Tal and Orly Morag, "School Visits to Natural History Museums: Teaching or Enriching?," *Journal of Research in Science Teaching* 44, no. 5 (2007): 747-769; Lynn Uyen Tran, "The Roles and Goals of Educators Teaching Science in Non-Formal Settings," *Mathematics, Science, and Technology Education* (Raleigh: North Carolina State University, 2002).
20. Heather King, "Supporting Natural History Enquiry in an Informal Setting: A Study of Museum Explainer Practice," *Department of Education and Professional Studies*, vol. PhD, (London: King's College London, 2009).
21. Kevin Crowley et al., "Shared Scientific Thinking in Everyday Parent-Child Activity," *Science Education* 85, no. 6 (2001): 712-32; Richard E. Grandy, "Constructivism and Objectivity: Disentangling Metaphysics from Pedagogy," *Science and Education* 6, no. 1-2 (1997): 43-53; Heather King, "Supporting Natural History Enquiry in an Informal Setting: A Study of Museum Explainer Practice," *Department of Education and Professional Studies*, vol. PhD, (London: King's College London, 2009); David Klahr and Milena Nigam, "The Equivalence of Learning Paths in Early Science Instruction: Effects of Direct Instruction and Discovery Learning," *Psychological Science* 15, no. 10 (2004): 661-667.
22. Donald A. Schön, *The Reflective Practitioner: How Professionals Think in Action*, (Basic Books, 1983).
23. Lynn Uyen Tran and Heather King, "The Professionalization of Museum Educators: The Case in Science Museums," *Museum Management and Curatorship* 22, no. 2 (2007): 129-147.
24. June Clark, "A Language for Nursing," *Nursing Standard* 13, no. 31 (1999): 42-47; David H. Hargreaves, "Teaching as a Research Based Profession: Possibilities and Prospects" (paper presented at The Teacher Training Agency Annual Lecture, London).
25. Lynn Uyen Tran, "Professionalization of Educators in Science Museums and Centers: Towards a Shared Language," *Journal of Science Communication* 7, no. 4 (2008): 1-6.

References

Bailey, E.B., "Researching Museum Educators' Perceptions of Their Roles, Identity, and Practice," in *Journal of Museum Education* (Museum Education Roundtable, 2006).

_____, "The Professional Relevance of Museum Educators," in *Journal of Museum Education* (Museum Education Roundtable, 2006).

Bitgood, S., B. Serrell, and D. Thompson, "The Impact of Informal Education on Visitors to Museums," in *Informal Science Learning: What the Research Says about Television, Science Museums, and Community-Based Projects*, ed. Crane, V., M. Chen, S. Bitgood, B. Serrell, D. Thompson, H. Nicholson, F. Weiss and P. Campbell (Dedham, MA: Research Communications, 1994).

Brüninghaus-Knubel, C., "Museum Education in the Context of Museum Functions," in *Running a Museum: A Practical Handbook*, ed. Boylan, P.J. (Paris, France: ICOM - International Council of Museums, 2006).

Calderhead, J., "Stimulated Recall: A Method for Research on Teaching," in *British Journal of Educational Psychology* (1981).

Carson, S., M. Shih, and E. Langer, "Sit Still and Pay Attention?," in *Journal of Adult Development* (2001).

Castle, M.C., "Interpreters, Docents, and Educators: Ways of Knowing, Ways of Teaching in a History Museum, an Art Gallery, and a Nature Centre," in *Curriculum, Teaching, and Learning* (Toronto: University of Toronto, 2001).

Clark, J., "A Language for Nursing," in *Nursing Standard* (1999).

Crowley, K., M.A. Callanan, J.L. Jipson, J. Galco, K. Topping, and J. Shrager, "Shared Scientific Thinking in Everyday Parent-Child Activity," in *Science Education* (2001).

Csikszentmihalyi, M. and K. Hermanson, "Intrinsic Motivation in Museums: What Makes Visitors Want to Learn?," *Museums News* (1995).

Eberbach, C. and K. Crowley, "From Living to Virtual: Learning from Museum Objects," *Curator* (2005).

Falk, J.H., W.W. Martin, and J.D. Balling, "The Novel Field Trip Phenomenon: Adjustment to Novel Settings Interferes with Task Learning," in *Journal of Research in Science Teaching* (1978).

Grandy, R.E., "Constructivism and Objectivity: Disentangling Metaphysics from Pedagogy," *Science and Education* (1997).

Hargreaves, D.H., "Teaching as a Research Based Profession: Possibilities and Prospects," *The Teacher Training Agency Annual Lecture* (London: The Teacher Training Agency, 1996).

Henry, B., "The Educator at the Crossroads of Institutional Change," *Journal of Museum Education* (2006).

Hohenstein, J.M. and L.U. Tran, "The Use of Questions in Exhibit Labels to Generate Explanatory Conversation Among Science Museum Visitors," *International Journal of Science Education* (2007).

Hooper-Greenhill, E., *Museum and Gallery Education* (Leicester: Leicester University Press, 1991).

King, H., "Supporting Natural History Enquiry in an Informal Setting: A Study of Museum Explainer Practice," *Department of Education and Professional Studies* (London: King's College London, 2009).

Kirschner, P.A., J. Sweller, and R.E. Clark, "Why Minimal Guidance During Instruction Does Not Work: An Analysis of the Failure of Constructivist, Discovery, Problem-Based, Experiential, and Inquiry-Based Teaching," *Educational Psychologist* (2006).

Klahr, D. and M. Nigam, "The Equivalence of Learning Paths in Early Science Instruction: Effects of Direct Instruction and Discovery Learning," *Psychological Science* (2004).

Leinhardt, G. and K. Crowley, "Objects of Learning, Objects of Talk: Changing Minds in Museums," *Perspectives on Object-Centered Learning in Museums*, ed. Paris, S.G. (Mahwah, NJ: Lawrence Erlbaum Associates, 2002).

Lyle, J., "Stimulated Recall: A Report on its Use in Naturalistic Research," *British Educational Research Journal* (2003).

Macdonald, S., "Exhibitions and Public Understanding of Science Paradox," *The Pantaneto Forum* (Luton, England: 2004).

McManus, P.M., "It's the Company You Keep: The Social Determination of Learning-Related Behavior in a Science Museum," *The International Journal of Museum Management and Curatorship* (1987).

Orosz, J.J. *Curators and Culture: The Museum Movement of America, 1740-1870,* (Tuscaloosa: University of Alabama Press, 1990).

Roberts, L.C. *From Knowledge to Narrative: Educators and the Changing Museum,* (Washington, DC: Smithsonian Institution Press, 1997).

Schauble, L., M. Gleason, R. Lehrer, K. Bartlett, A. Petrosino, A. Allen, K. Clinton, E. Ho, M. Jones, Y.-S. Lee, J.-A. Phillips, J. Siegler, and J. Street, "Supporting Science Learning in Museums," *Learning Conversations in Museums,* ed. Leinhardt, G., K. Crowley and K. Knutson (Mahwah, NJ: Lawrence Erlbaum Associates, 2002).

Schön, D.A. *The Reflective Practitioner: How Professionals Think in Action,* (Basic Books, 1983).

Tal, T. and O. Morag, "School Visits to Natural History Museums: Teaching or Enriching?," *Journal of Research in Science Teaching* (2007).

Tran, L.U., "Professionalization of Educators in Science Museums and Centers: Towards a Shared Language," *Journal of Science Communication* (2008).

_____. "Teaching Science in Museums: The Pedagogy and Goals of Museum Educators," *Science Education* (2007).

_____. "The Roles and Goals of Educators Teaching Science in Non-Formal Settings," *Mathematics, Science, and Technology Education* (Raleigh: North Carolina State University, 2002).

_____. "The Work of Science Museum Educators," *Museum Management and Curatorship* (2008).

Tran, L.U. and H. King, "Knowledge Informing the Actions: The Professional Practice of Science Museum Educators," (in progress).

_____. "The Professionalization of Museum Educators: The Case in Science Museums," *Museum Management and Curatorship* (2007).

Lynn Uyen Tran is an educational researcher with the Lawrence Hall of Science. She has a Ph.D. in science education from North Carolina State University and has done her post-doctoral work with the Center for Informal Learning and Schools at King's College London. She conducts research and professional development on the knowledge, identity, and work of science educators in museums.

Heather King is an independent consultant specializing in museum education. She gained her Ph.D. in science education from King's College London, where she was also the Director for the Center for Informal Learning and Schools. Her particular research interests focus on the role of museum explainers and their support of natural history inquiry.

A Scenario for the Future of Museum Educators

Mary Kay Cunningham

Abstract   More than any other staff member, museum educators'
knowledge and experience working with visitors make them uniquely
qualified to take on leadership roles as museums transform themselves
into lifelong learning organizations. The article encourages museum educators to initiate discussions about change by offering a fictional scenario
of future leadership roles and a framework of relevant questions challenging educators, along with other staff, to begin their own organizational transformation.

"...if we worry that there's a shortage of leaders, we're just looking in the
wrong place, usually at the top of some hierarchy. Instead, we need to look
around us, to look locally. And we need to look at ourselves."
Margaret Wheatley[1]

Our world is changing rapidly. When global travel, communication, and media
were limited, it was enough for museums to offer information and artifacts
that expanded our access to unknown culture, history, science, or art forms.
But with innovations like the worldwide web and social media, visitors want
and need opportunities to contribute to a dialogue with the museum and each
other—to personalize the experience for themselves and to be a part of
something with others. This means that museums must continue to evolve.

We anticipate the day, perhaps soon, when our museums' successes will
no longer be measured solely by the extent of their collections and research,
nor even by the numbers of visitors who participate in programs or events,
but additionally and significantly by our ability to serve, engage, and enrich
our communities. As museums shift towards being more visitor-centered
and maintaining relevancy by forging connections with our communities,

Journal of Museum Education, Volume 34, Number 2, Summer 2009, pp. 163–170.
163

they will require strong leadership. Museum educators are uniquely suited to lead this change.[2]

Every day the front-line interactions of educators double as regular focus groups with our target audiences and provide rich insights about what people want and need from our institutions. We know first-hand the richness of their learning conversations, the depth of their connections, and the power of an "a-ha" moment. This knowledge is power.

Museum educators must seize this opportunity to leverage our knowledge of learning and experiences with visitors to make ourselves indispensible in this time of change. If we are to remain relevant and continue evolving, it is not enough for educators to focus on advancing our skills as facilitators of quality learning experiences. We must also consider how our particular expertise qualifies us for leadership roles while museums prepare to transform themselves into responsive institutions that customize visitor experiences.[3] As museums become, in fact, lifelong learning organizations.

Change of this scale will require that we fundamentally alter the way we operate. Beyond the rhetoric of calling ourselves "educational institutions" and claims of being "visitor-centered," we must commit to becoming learning organizations *internally* as well as externally. Creating exemplary learning experiences for visitors begins by encouraging and supporting museum staff as lifelong learners.

Throughout this edition of the *Journal*, we argue that if museums are to succeed, they must become the learning organizations Peter Senge describes in his book *The Fifth Discipline: The Art & Practice of the Learning Organization* (2006), "where people continually expand their capacity to create the desired results; where new patterns of thinking are nurtured; where collective aspiration is set free; where people are continually learning to see the whole together." But what does that look like in practice? Try to picture the following in your own museum, as part of your own day.

A SAMPLING OF FUTURE ROLES FOR MUSEUM EDUCATORS[4]

An hour before the museum's doors are opened, museum educators are already fulfilling their role as facilitators of learning—both anticipating and planning for experiences with visitors and, equally important, supporting learning among the staff in their institution and in the broader field of museum education.

Before preparing for daily programs on the floor, Andrew logs onto OLLME (Online Learning Laboratory for Museum Educators—a **free digital repository for practical tools and information**) to watch videos of educators from other museums facilitating a program that he had shared via OLLME a month earlier. This exchange inspired Andrew to try new techniques and made him feel a part of a community. This video was one of many items on his OLLME queue that he looked forward to reviewing during his weekly allotted time for professional development.

Elizabeth, responsible for job-embedded, museum-wide professional development, begins her monthly shared learning experience for staff managers in all divisions of the museum. Based on observations of their work and conversations with each manager about their needs, today's seminar offers tools for managers to support their staff in a **critical reflection of their work and developing their own measures of success**. Later that day, Elizabeth will meet with Akari, a newly hired educator, for cognitive coaching[5] to develop goals for increasing his own knowledge about facilitating free-choice learning.

For next month's manager professional development, David and Kate, two experienced museum educators, will facilitate a dialogue on the social nature of learning in museums. This exercise is an excerpt of the larger collaborative learning seminar they offer internally for volunteer and staff museum educators and externally as **consultants for other museum's front-line staff**. They document their methods from these seminars and **measure the impact** of the new facilitation strategies on visitor learning in a variety of institutions in hopes of **publishing** their results by the end of the year.

Lisha leads an **interdisciplinary team** of staff from the Visitor Learning Division (staff from education, experience and exhibit development, visitor studies, and social media) in prototyping a new facilitator-friendly[6] exhibit. After months of **collaborating** at every stage of **interpretive planning** and design, the team awaits the arrival of Gladys, a skilled volunteer facilitator, who will test the exhibit with visitors during the **evaluation** today.

Carlos was already on his video conference with the principal of a nearby middle school and the director of the Boys & Girls Club finalizing their joint **grant proposal**. Their **partnership** promised an alternative model for meeting the school's learning targets while offering enrichment programs connecting these children and their families to life-long learning outside the classroom. Just last week Carlos had made his case for the need for such a program when he accompanied the museum's director to **lobby the state's legislature** about the importance of funding learning experiences in museums.

In the Visitor Experience Design Center, Leah and Jasmine check postings for activities and exhibits available at the museum that day. The Center exists to **support visitors in customizing their experience** using the tenets of participatory design[7] and to **initiate a relationship between the staff and visitors** that grows with repeat visitation. Using data from past visitors and individualized preferences and group needs[8] entered by the visitor, the Experience Design program produces a prioritized list of recommendations for experiences most likely to offer the highest impact. Leah's role today included guiding visitors through the program and discussing recommendations. Jasmine was already chatting electronically with one of the "Community Designers" (members) planning their visit from home. During their correspondence, she solicits ideas for new programs and exhibits and personally invites them to an upcoming experience uniquely matched to their interests and abilities.

More than just highlighting the possible ways educators might lead, the scenario depicts a museum that is "learning to see the whole together"—a future where *learning*, both for the visitor and staff of the museum, is the unifying agent for everyone working to create a powerful visitor experience. An active learning community is created in the museum that both models and supports the learning we want to foster in our visitors.

Now consider the bolded text above which emphasizes the many ways museum educators might be able to increase the relevancy and public value of the institution as a learning organization. In the scenario we see museum educators:

1. **Deepening their own understanding** of how to be successful, empowered, and fulfilled by their daily work as museum educators

2. **Overseeing job-embedded, museum-wide professional development** centered on individually set performance goals and building staff capacity to support visitor learning
3. **Sharing expertise and exchanging information** to enhance their knowledge and credibility in the field and contribute to common knowledge, language and practice
4. **Leading cross-departmental learning and planning groups** to maximize potential of the institution to fulfill its' mission and bolster internal value for learning
5. **Developing strategic partnerships** with community and **serving as an advocate** of free-choice learning to harnesses financial support
6. **Preparing to facilitate peak learning experiences** that are customized to meet the needs of the visitor and employing the proven practices of successful free-choice learning

These various roles are natural extensions of the work we already engage in as museum educators. In addition to our commitment to educating the public, we have the skills to educate vertically for our administrators, and horizontally to others in the institution. Fostering lifelong learning (for both visitors and staff) is not only instrumental to sustaining a learning organization,[9] but an opportunity for museum educators to apply their skills and deepen their own practice. These kinds of experiences will offer much needed reward and incentive for educators to remain engaged (rather than switching professions) to become the future leaders within our institutions.

In light of heavy workloads and unforgiving schedules, it is asking a lot for educators to take on leadership roles. But if those of us most passionate about learning do not step forward to advocate for this transformation, who will? Knowing where to start can be overwhelming, but simplify the task by temporally ignoring future unknowns (time, funding, etc) and challenge yourself to simply start a conversation about change.

Begin by creating your own think tank. When considering who might participate ask:

- Who will constructively challenge and expand my ideas about the future?
- Beyond education staff, who can serve as representatives from all roles involved in visitor learning (exhibits, visitor studies, etc)?
- Are there other stakeholders that could contribute to the conversation? Volunteers, teachers, members, visitor groups, advocacy organizations?

Next, begin dreaming about the future. If we know we need to change, we must acknowledge what is known about our current (and past) practice, but devote our energy devising what we want our museums to be in the future. As Tony Wagner writes, "Your system--any system--is perfectly designed to produce the results you're getting."[10] Subsequently, since the current systems in our museums are not delivering what we (or our visitors) want and need, then how can we reshape our values (or revisit the mission of the institution) and systems to support becoming a learning organization? Consider the following questions (posed from the perspective of your institution):

- What data will we need to collect to promote advancements and measure our success as a learning organization? What would be our criteria for success?
- How might the mission or core values/beliefs of the organization need to change for our museum to value the work (in addition to the outputs) of becoming a learning organization?
- What would working in our museum look like if it were truly a learning organization? How would our roles and interactions be different than today?
- How would the all staff and departments involved with visitor learning work together?
- How might we share our experience with others in the field beyond the current methods of publications and conference presentations?
- What kinds of experiences, responsibilities, and support will keep us engaged and rewarded in our work?

While there may be examples of museums already operating or providing learning experiences as described in the scenario, it is not enough to say, "let's be more like *them*." Each institution must chart a course and undergo a change process that empowers[11] staff to create experiences by building on their expertise and intuition, while meeting the needs of their unique audiences. These questions are just the beginning of a journey towards becoming learning organizations.[12]

Some members of the museum field who helped shape this article echo our new president, talking less about the need for a definitive set of skills to facilitate change and more about the need for a "set of curiosities"[13] to guide us; less about having everyone reach agreement around the table, and more about creating our own "team of rivals"[14] that can create a thoughtful dialogue about what the future should be.

As leaders in this transformation to being a learning organization we don't have to have the answers, we just have to initiate the experience of learning together by inviting diverse perspectives to a conversation, doing our best thinking, promoting innovation, advocating for time to test the most promising of ideas, encouraging change based on our findings, and continuing the learning conversation--regardless of the results.

In times of change, learners inherit the Earth, while the learned find themselves beautifully equipped to deal with a world that no longer exists. *Eric Hoffer*

Notes

1. Margaret Wheatley, *Turning To One Another*, 2nd edition. (San Francisco: Berrett-Koehler, 2009).
2. See additional discussion of educator's role in leading change in several articles in Fall 2008 issue of *Journal of Museum Education*. Especially the article by Jennifer Wild Czajkowski and Shirlee Hudson Hill, "Transformation and Interpretation; What is the Museum Educator's Role?"
3. There are too many references to list here, but a rich resource of information about visitor experiences and future trends can be found in the following publications:

   John H. Falk and Beverly K. Sheppard, *Thriving In the Knowledge Age: New Business Models for Museums and Other Cultural Institutions* (Lanham, MD: Rowman/AltaMira, 2006).

   Stephanie Weaver, *Creating Great Visitor Experiences; A Guide for Museums, Parks, Zoos, Gardens, & Libraries.* (Walnut Creek, CA: Left Coast Press, 2007).

   Mary Ellen Munley, et al., "Envisioning A Customized Museum: An Agenda to Guide Reflective Practice and Research" *In Principle In Practice; Museums as Learning Institutions* (Lanham, MD: Rowman/AltaMira, 2007):77-90.

   Tasmin Astor-Jack, et al., "Investigating Socially Mediated Learning" *In Principle In Practice; Museums as Learning Institutions* (Lanham, MD: Rowman/AltaMira, 2007): 217-228.
4. The scenario was created with the help of my own think tank comprised of museum and school administrators, university faculty, exhibit developers, researchers, consultants, and current and former front-line educators. Their ideas, hopes, and even cautionary tales all resulted in this vision for the future. Endless thanks to Lynn Dierking, John Falk, David Ebitz, Erik Holland, Scott Pattison, Lynn Uyen Tran, Stephanie Weaver, Julie Smith, David Perry, David Snyder, Kim Aziz, Dan Moeller, Mary Roberts and especially Mark Larson and Tina Nolan.
5. Cognitive Coaching involves offering tools for stimulating reflection of one's own practice that enables the professional to develop their own plan for development and problem solving.(www.cognitivecoaching.com)
6. Mary Kay Cunningham and Scott Pattison, "Fostering Facilitation: Designing Exhibits and Training Staff for Conversational Interpretation" *National Association for Interpretation's Proceedings Collections 2006-2008.* (Fort Collins, CO, InterpPress 2008). Please feel free to contact the author for a PDF of this article at *marykay@visitordialogue.com.*
7. See Nina Simon's upcoming book on Participatory Design with supporting information at http://museumtwo.blogspot.com/2009/02/what-do-you-need-to-make-argument-for.html.

8. Learn more about identities and needs of visitors in John Falk's new book, *Identity and the Museum Visitor Experience* (Left Coast Press, 2009) and for family groups, *Family Learning in Museums: The PISEC Perspective* (PISEC 1998)
9. Michael Fullan "Understanding Change", *The Jossey-Bass Reader on Educational Leadership* (San Francisco, CA: Jossey-Bass Press: 2007) :170
10. Tony Wagner, *Change Leadership; a Practical Guide to Transforming Our Schools* (San Francisco, CA: Jossey-Bass 2006): 106
11. For excellent article on impacts of empowerment and cultural change in institutions see Mary Theresa Seig and Ken Bubp's article, "The Culture of Empowerment; Driving and Sustaining Change at Conner Prairie" *Curator* 51/2. (April 2008): 208.
12. The last article in this issue of the *Journal*, "The Leader's Bookshelf "will offer an annotated bibliography of resources that will provide tools or examples for how to craft a path for becoming a learning organization.
13. Specific term used in personal communications with John Falk, February 2009.
14. Reference to Doris Kearns Goodwin's book, *Team of Rivals; The Political Genius of Abraham Lincoln* (Simon & Schuster 2005)

References

Falk, John H. and Beverly K. Sheppard, *Thriving in the Knowledge Age: New Business Models for Museums and Other Cultural Institutions* (Lanham, MD: AltaMira Press, 2006).
Munley, Mary Ellen, and Randy Roberts, "Are Museum Educators Still Necessary?" *Journal of Museum Education* 31, no.1 (Spring 2006).

Mary Kay Cunningham is an independent museum professional with over 15 years experience working with museums and cultural institutions. Her company, Dialogue, works to improve visitor learning experiences through collaborative seminars about conversational interpretation and facilitating visitor experience planning. Mary Kay is the author of The Interpreters Training Manual for Museums, a best-selling book published by the American Association of Museums in 2004. She can be contacted at marykay@visitordialogue.com.

From the Margins to the Center
Recommendations for Current
and Aspiring Educational Leaders

Tina R. Nolan

Abstract Tina Nolan presents a call to action for current and future leaders to assume a new role as change leaders for the museum education profession. This article puts forth a series of recommendations and strategies for repositioning museum educators from the margins of their institutions to the center. Included among these recommendations are literature suggestions, guiding questions for self-reflection and journaling, and group activities intended to offer a new lens from which to view the profession.

Kate Hawthorne[1] thought she'd made it. After years of struggling to find her niche, this 27-year-old, well-educated young woman thought she'd finally found a job that tapped into her passion for the environment, her love of museums, and her desire to make a difference in people's lives. Kate started as a docent to build her resume, was hired by the education department soon thereafter to lead teens programming, and served on the museum environmental committee. It was not long before she was promoted to a new position: Coordinator of Green Initiatives. Kate's job included, among other things, liaising with the community around the museum to promote green practice, working with other environmental organizations to partner on green events throughout the city, and promoting the mission of her science museum. She was golden--for about three months. In October 2008 museums across the country began to feel the pinch of the economic crisis. Kate's position was eliminated along with several other education and guest service positions. The education department was split apart; managers, coordinators and educators were laid off, and the remaining public programs staff was shifted from the education department to the guest services department. Who was charged to guide the public programs staff in their work? The manager of the gift shop. The message in this museum was clear. In tough economic times, nonessential expenses are the first to go, and the education department had become a nonessential expense. Most unfortunate of all is the fact that this story is not unusual.

What will it take to reposition museum educators from the margins of our institutions to the center? It will require a movement within the profession--thousands of people willing to invest time, energy and resources to carve out a new identity and raise the professional bar. And it will take leaders to mobilize them and guide the way. By "leaders," I'm not referring exclusively to managers or directors or vice-presidents. No, those kinds of leaders already exist. They struggle bravely and mightily for their staff, shielding them as best they can from unrealistic mandates, grappling with increased pressure from senior staff and trustees for more "WOW" experiences and dealing with ever-tightening budgets requiring them to do more with less. The type of museum education leader I am referring to is the leader who can imagine a museum of the future and a set of educational responsibilities, positions and opportunities which don't currently exist.

Museum educators will require *educational leadership* if they are to play a role in shaping the future museums of America. What is an educational leader? An educational leader is one who understands the practice and pedagogy of museum educators. They understand leadership principles such as organizational culture change and systems thinking. They have reflected deeply on their core values and stand by them, and they know how to mobilize others to lead. An educational leader knows how best to manage staff, but also understands that management is only one part of a much larger job. An educational leader places the highest value on the educational mission of the institution, endeavors to be the lead-learner, and is unafraid of taking risks and leading change.

What follows is an initial set of recommendations and strategies for current and aspiring leaders to consider as methods for repositioning themselves and their staff from the margins of their institution to the center. The concepts and frameworks explored in this article offer only a starting point, though. There are entire graduate and doctoral programs devoted to learning about organizational culture, change theory, and other leadership principles. As a former Director of Education at a museum in Chicago, I empathize with current and aspiring leaders during this difficult time in our field. Having spent the last three years studying educational leadership concepts, I have had the luxury of testing them in different types of cultural institutions. I have also been afforded opportunities to talk with museum educators and their leaders across the country about leadership and the current state of our profession. I offer these suggestions to begin a dialogue among the profession about leadership and, hopefully, to elicit change. There is much work to be done and ample opportunity to pioneer a new future for the museum educators we serve.

Recommendation One:
Read the Latest Literature on Leadership and Change

If you search through museum-related literature, you will find books on leadership written for museum Presidents, CEOs and Trustees. While you may not be at the helm of your institution, the same leadership principles apply to museum educators as to your CEO. Even if you are not the head of your department there is leadership opportunity for those who aspire to lead. Think of yourself as a leader or an emerging leader and begin to delve into the literature and build your foundation.

If you haven't done so already, *begin examining the literature that envisions a new future for museums* as educational and public service endeavors, such as *Excellence and Equity: Education and the Public Dimension of Museums*[2], now in its third edition, or Bonnie Pitman's *Presence of Mind: Museums and the Spirit of Learning*[3]. Combine that with an *exploration of museum related literature focused on the foundations of leadership*. In *Hesselbein On Leadership*[4], Frances Hesselbein stresses that leadership is about character and about understanding "how to be" as opposed to "how to do it." As many of the leadership books will tell you, leading from within yourself is the best place to start. Sherene Suchy's book, *Leading With Passion: Change Management in the 21st-Century Museum*[5] focuses on the importance of nurturing relationships, building trust, and understanding the change process. Such principles extend beyond the walls of the museum and permeate leadership literature regardless of organization type.

Examine leadership in places of learning. We are (or were, or aspire to be), after all, leaders in departments centered on creating opportunities for the public to learn. We may be in an exhibits department, or an education department; a technology department or a volunteer department. In many small institutions we are all these departments rolled into one. It does not matter where our audiences learn, and it does not matter what your title is, the focus of the work is on the visitor as a learner. Look at the wealth of literature centered on leading in places where people learn and you will quickly find that there already exist sets of leadership best practices, frameworks and protocols for leading those who craft experiences or facilitate learning. These practices can be easily adapted or reframed to suit the needs of educators in museums. In his book, *Leadership for Learning: How to Help Teachers Succeed,*[6] Carl Glickman has a created a clinical supervision protocol for new and veteran teachers which includes a non-judgmental and collaborative approach to conducting observations. I have tested it myself in museum and outdoor learning settings (in both formal and informal programs) and have found it to be invaluable in empowering educators to examine their own practice. Models for lesson study and walk-throughs, for action research and data analysis, for empowering parents to learn with their children have all been created for schooling and should be examined for use in other places of learning. It is a terrific starting point, and the opportunities to craft new museum-specific protocols and tools abound.

Recommendation Two: Examine the Culture of Your Organization and Be Willing to Lead Change, If Necessary

There are any numbers of specific leadership concepts to explore, but I recommend you start by *examining the culture of your organization first.* Roland Barth explained school culture this way, and his definition can easily be applied to the museum world:

> Every school has a culture. Some are hospitable, others toxic. A school's culture can work for or against improvement and reform. Some schools are populated by teachers and administrators who are reformers, others by sheep, others by educators who are gifted and talented at subverting reform. . . . To change culture requires that we be first aware of the culture, the way things are here.[7]

Unless you have a clear picture of the existing culture of your organization, both within your department and without, and can muster up the courage it will take to change the culture if necessary, any innovation you try is not likely to be sustained. Understanding culture and, just as important, *understanding how to change culture* is imperative.

How does one change the culture of an organization? Start by *examining the systems that drive the organization itself.* Such an examination must include an analysis of how the systems in your institution overlap, interrelate, and impact each other.

Peter Senge became famous for writing about systems thinking in his well-known book, *The Fifth Discipline.* In the second edition of the *Jossey-Bass Reader on Educational Leadership,*[8] Senge revised his initial thinking and articulated an operational framework for organizations that, if mastered, can lead to innovation. In a nutshell, Senge defines each of the four best practices in business models:

Personal Mastery—the discipline of continually clarifying and deepening our personal vision, of focusing our energies, of developing patience, and of seeing reality objectively

Mental Models—deeply engrained generalizations, or even pictures or images that influence how we understand the world and how we take action

Building a Shared Vision—the skill of unearthing shared "pictures of the future" that foster genuine commitment and enrollment rather than compliance

Team Learning—the capacity of members of a team to suspend assumptions and enter into a genuine "thinking together"[9]

Systems Thinking is the practice of integrating the disciplines, fusing them into a coherent body of theory and practice. Senge argues that looking within and across each discipline to develop them in concert with one another will help to foster learning and change over time.

How might this work in your setting? Try this next activity with a group of colleagues and see what you find. Begin by identifying the systems in your organization, and then look across each of these systems to see how they interrelate. You can start by placing the systems of your institution into bigger "buckets," such as:

Operational/Logistical Systems: These systems refer to the facility itself. Given the complexity of departments, range and types of visitors, and the changing visitation patterns throughout any given year, operational thinking is likely something you spend much of your time doing already. The key here is to unearth *dysfunctional* mental models by asking questions that require some thought be given to the impact of operations on *other systems* like the instructional support systems and the visitor support systems. Why do we do things the way we do them? Are we doing them to enable the visitor to have a positive learning experience, or are we doing them for the convenience of the people who work in the building? Are there any sacred cows here? If so, it's time to re-think those systems.

Instructional Support Systems for Educators: These systems refer to the ways in which team learning and personal mastery occur. Do you have mentoring programs, a supervision plan, a professional development plan? How do you and your colleagues, both individually and as a collective, continue to grow, learn, and share?

Visitor Support Systems: What systems support visitor learning? Where does this learning occur and how? Who is responsible for visitor learning and what systems are in place to check in about whether or not visitors are actually learning? How are the results of your findings disseminated throughout the organization?

Program/Exhibit Development Support Systems: How are programs (both formal and informal) developed? How often do educators come together to share content-related development across the different audiences (e.g. prairie plant adaptations interpreted to teachers, to families, to young children)? How do educators engage across departments in exhibit development and testing? How are exhibits and programs utilized in concert? How is data about visitor learning (quantitative, qualitative, anecdotal, etc.) collected and used to inform decisions?

Once you've identified the systems in your museum ask yourself these questions:

1. In what ways are the systems interconnected within and between "buckets"?
2. Are any of these systems broken? What impact might the broken systems have on other systems? Example: the exhibits department is scheduled to temporarily close an exhibit for maintenance on the same day a major community event is to take place in that space. Can you think of other examples in your institution and examine them through this lens?
3. Think about a part of the system. Choose one system that works well. Why does it work well?

Once you've begun to look at the systems in your building, looking across systems and within systems, you will see patterns and places for improvement. You will also begin to more fully understand the culture of your department and your institution.

Recommendation Three:
Craft Your Personal Identity as a Leader

Ask any good leader about how they became so effective and they will tell you that they spent time exploring their own values and beliefs. *They created a personal vision for themselves* in their work and they live by that vision. In order to effect innovative and sustainable change within your institution, you must take time to understand yourself as a leader. Self reflection is the key. You can begin by asking these questions:

1. What are your core values?
2. What do you stand for?
3. If you could run your department and/or your institution any way you wanted to, what would it look like? How would it look for your colleagues, and for the visitor?

Draw on what you have read about leadership as you begin to *define or redefine your leadership characteristics.* Journal about what you read, even if you think you are not a good writer. Reflect on your thinking and writing, revise, and write some more. Let others you trust implicitly read what you have written. Begin a dialogue about leadership. You will soon start to see the areas you feel are your strengths, so build on those. Are you one who builds alliances? If so, create structures to enable others in your department to form alliances in your institution both within your department and among the wider institution. Are you at your best when you are mentoring others, either formally or informally? If so, create a structure for mentoring within your department, build capacity in others to become proficient at mentoring, evaluate your program, and make revisions as necessary. Write about it and share your model with the rest of the museum world.

Build upon your strengths and then move on to the things that are more challenging for you. For example, if you feel less secure about budgeting, stretch yourself in new ways to build your capacity in this area. Talk to other budget heads in your institution about how they do it. Talk to people outside your institution and explore their perspectives. Find other literature on museum finance and study it to build a stronger foundation for yourself in this work. Do not be afraid to show that you are learning in this area. Be the lead learner in your department or organization.

How will you be able to do all these things when you do not even have time for lunch on any given day? Look to literature that helps you build your own capacity for leadership without succumbing to burn-out or chronic stress. In other words, change the way in which you approach your work. *Strive for resonance.*

In their latest book, *Resonant Leadership*[10], Richard Boyatzis and Annie McKee argue that organizations with leaders who create and sustain resonance will be most able to succeed in a rapidly changing world. What is a resonant leader? Boyatzis and McKee describe them this way:

> ... resonant leaders manage their emotions well and read individuals and groups accurately. They consciously attune to people, focus them on a common cause, build a sense of community, and create a climate that enables people to tap into passion, energy, and a desire to move together in a positive direction. They are optimistic and realistic at the same time.[11]

The definition above encompasses what Boyatzis and McKee state are the three most important qualities a resonant leader must cultivate. They must be mindful of themselves and others, they must be hopeful even in the face of despair, and they must be compassionate. Boyatzis and McKee draw on brain research to show how nurturing mindfulness, hope, and compassion enable the brain and other organs in the body to better cope with stress. Stress will always be a part of leading; the challenge is to keep from suffering under chronic stress by creating for yourself a cycle of renewal.

Recommendation Four: Create a Learning Organization

The most successful organizations are learning organizations be they Google, Pixar/Disney Company, Whole Foods Market, Stevenson High School, or the Connor Prairie Living History Museum. The keys to a successful learning organization are that the learning is centered on a shared vision, there are shared definitions of the work, and the work is tied directly to a larger moral purpose. In the case of Connor Prairie, the *entire organization shifted its focus away from the old ways of doing business and toward the visitor as a learner.* Together they utilized research-based strategies at all levels of the organization, collected data about visitor learning, and shared that data across the institution to inform every decision. The model created by Connor Prairie was awarded and IMLS National Leadership Grant, which enabled them to disseminate their model through the creation of a DVD entitled *Opening the Doors to Great Guest Experiences* (2007).[12]

To what extent does the staff in your institution learn together? To what extent does your institution use the results of research-based data collection to make decisions? To what extent does your institution involve staff at every level, and to what extent is your department leading the way about visitor learning? Peter Senge describes how leaders can lead learning organizations when he writes:

> A resonant leader who thinks systemically, understands the culture of their organization, and understands how to change culture is ready to do the work of creating a learning organization, [which is] an organization that is continually expanding its capacity to create its future. For such an organization, it is not enough to merely survive. "Survival learning," or what is more often termed as "adaptive learning," is important—indeed it is necessary. But for a learning organization, "adaptive learning" must be joined by "generative learning," learning that enhances our capacity to create.[13]

Recommendation Five: Understand, Shape, and Articulate a New Role and Identity for Your Fellow Museum Educators

The most effective leaders view themselves as individuals who serve the people they represent. This is not lip service but rather an earned leadership which is bestowed upon the leader by the led. What better way to serve your staff, to earn their trust, to move them from the margins to the center, than to *build their capacity and advocate for them* on their behalf? Start by drawing on and adding to the newly emerging literature on the practice and pedagogy of museum educators. As Lynn Uyen Tran and Heather King have advised in this edition of the *Journal*, obtaining a more complete understanding of the museum educator's practice will aid in the creation of a shared language across institution type, which will lead to less fragmented discourse across the field and toward more public recognition of the field as a profession.

The most effective leaders also empower museum educators as critical elements within their institution. You can accomplish this by *distributing leadership across your department*. But don't confuse distributed leadership with signing your staff up to participate on committees. Distribute leadership based on the strengths of others--not by the tasks that need to get done, or by what the organizational chart shows. For example, if you have a staff member who holds particular expertise on writing label copy and developing on-line activities, do not send them to represent the department at a meeting about what should go in the gift shop. Ask them to attend a meeting having to do with the content of a particular exhibit instead. While they might have a few things to say about the educational appropriateness of some of the items in the gift shop, they will have much more input about visitor learning at an exhibit design meeting. They will lend their expertise as opposed to showing up as a representative of the department. If you have a staff member who coordinates school group visits, and excels at thinking operationally, don't send them to a meeting about the content development of a new exhibit just because they are the School Programs Coordinator. Ask them to attend the meeting about the opening of the exhibit instead. Go one step further and ask the School Programs Coordinator to identify the related content area expert on their team and distribute the leadership around staff capacity building across your department.

The best leaders are unafraid of *mobilizing change agents*. Mobilize thousands of them, for it is in people, lots of people, where the momentum for change lies. David Ebitz, former Director of the Ringling Museum, provides a perfect example of how advocating on behalf of the work of his education staff enabled his institution to garner political support and money:

As advocates, museum leaders direct their attention outward. But do not forget to engage your own staff in the process of developing your messages and give them opportunities to participate in conveying them. A museum educator on the staff of the Ringling Museum surprised me with her suggestion that I call upon teachers from around the State of Florida who had participated in workshops at the Ringling to contact their local legislators and explain how the museum provided educational services for their local districts. It became one of the most effective tools in advocating for increased state government support for the museum.[14]

Museum educators, unbeknownst to many of them, hold a lot of power in their organizations. They are the voice and the face of the institution's mission. They are the human connection between the collections, the visitor, and the community outside the museum walls. They can measure quantitatively and qualitatively the impact they have on the learning experience, whether that experience is formal or informal. Good leaders can help them to realize the power that they have, marshal their collective expertise, give them a voice and shape their new role as critical stakeholders in the museum. I encourage you to scrutinize and test the recommendations in this article and examine your own leadership. Add to the recommendations, refine them, and identify strategies for building a new professional identity not just for yourselves, but for the future educational leaders you inspire.

Notes

1. The name of this individual has been changed to protect privacy.
2. American Association of Museums, *Excellence and Equity: Education and the Public Dimension of Museums* (Washington DC; 1992).
3. Pitman, Bonnie, ed., *Presence of Mind: Museums and the Spirit of Learning.* (Washington DC: American Association of Museums, 1999).
4. Frances Hesselbein, *Hesselbein on Leadership* (Boston: Jossey-Bass, 2008).
5. Serene Suchy, *Leading With Passion: Change Management in the 21st Century Museum* (Lanham, MD: AltaMira Press, 2008).
6. Carl D. Glickman, *Leadership for Learning: How to Help Teachers Succeed* (Alexandria, VA: Association for Supervision and Curriculum, 2002).
7. Roland Barth, *The Jossey-Bass Reader on Educational Leadership* (San Francisco: Jossey-Bass, 2007), 160.
8. Jossey-Bass, *The Jossey-Bass Reader on Educational Leadership* (San Francisco: Jossey-Bass, 2007).
9. Peter Senge, *The Jossey-Bass Reader on Educational Leadership* (San Francisco: Jossey-Bass, 2007), 3-10.
10. Richard Boyatzis and Annie McKee, *Resonant Leadership* (Boston: Harvard Business School Press, 2005).
11. Richard Boyatzis and Annie McKee, *Resonant Leadership* (Boston: Harvard Business School Press, 2005), 22.
12. DVD entitled *Opening the Doors to Great Guest Experiences* (2007), http://www.connerprairie.org/About-Us/Who-We-Are/Opening-Doors.aspx (accessed July 31, 2009).
13. Peter Senge, *The Jossey-Bass Reader on Educational Leadership* (San Francisco: Jossey-Bass, 2007), 13.
14. David Ebitz, "Purpose, Stakeholders and Values: Museum Leadership in the 21st Century," *Museology Quarterly*, 22(4), 53-75.

Tina Nolan (Tina.Nolan@nl.edu) has spent the past 16 years working as an educator in cultural institutions. In February 1999, Nolan helped to open the Chicago Academy of Sciences Peggy Notebaert Nature Museum. In 2000, Nolan was Manager of Student and Teacher Programs, and was named Director of Education at the Nature Museum in 2001. Nolan joined National-Louis University in 2006 as Associate Director of Partnerships in the National College of Education. In this capacity, Nolan establishes new partnerships between NLU's National College of Education and school districts, education reform organizations, cultural institutions and community organizations nationally and internationally. Nolan is also an adjunct faculty member at National-Louis University and is currently teaching graduate-level coursework in the Educational Leadership program. Nolan continues to work with museums and other not-for-profit educational organizations as an independent education consultant. Most recently, Nolan became a board member for the Museum Education Roundtable. Nolan has a Masters degree in Educational Leadership and is currently pursuing a doctorate in Education where the focus of her research is on educational leadership in cultural institutions.

The Leader's Bookshelf
Suggestions for Reading More About Change Leadership

Tina Nolan

In the fall 2006 issue of the *Journal of Museum Education* Dennis Schatz provided a list of reference materials on what he felt were new competencies required by all museum educators outside of their normal content area expertise: how to be competitive in an information and opportunity-rich environment, how to foster better collaboration, and how to achieve a more thorough understanding of how visitors learn in today's museums. Schatz argued that museum educators must be comfortable wearing many hats in order "for the contemporary museum educator to be successful."[1]

In this edition of the *Journal*, I called upon all the contributing authors to put forth their recommendations for essential readings centered on the three areas of leadership explored throughout this edition: **pedagogical leadership, organizational leadership, and change leadership**. The references listed below are intended to accompany the many additional literature references found within the articles in this journal. This is by no means an exhaustive list but rather, a place to start.

PEDAGOGICAL LEADERSHIP: GETTING STARTED RESOURCES

We have argued that educational leaders must not only understand how visitors learn in museum settings, but that they must also have a thorough understanding of what good teaching looks like in a museum. To that end, I have adapted a term commonly used among school superintendents and principals—instructional leadership—and called it **pedagogical leadership**: leadership on the art and science of crafting and delivering learning experiences. Together, the authors and I have compiled a list of readings to get us started down the path of identifying good pedagogy. These references provide frameworks and strategies for fostering communities of educators who look

Journal of Museum Education, Volume 34, Number 2, Summer 2009, pp. 183-187.

closely at how museum educators teach, how they craft lessons, how they create exhibit experiences and take-home materials, etc. We suggest museum education leaders adapt some strategies used in school settings for use in non-school settings to help build leadership and new sets of best practice in this area.

Charlotte Danielson and Thomas L. McGreal, *Teacher Evaluation to Enhance Professional Practice* (Alexandria, VA: Association for Supervision and Curriculum Development and Educational Testing Service, 2000). Charlotte Danielson and Thomas McGreal, two nationally known experts on teacher professional development and education reform, reinvent teacher evaluation so that it becomes ongoing teacher professional development.

David Ebitz, "Qualifications and the Professional Preparation and Development of Art Museum Educators," *Studies in Art Education* 46 (2) 2005:150-169. Ebitz describes the initiatives developed by with the field of art museum education to raise the profile and ensure the caliber of art educators. He also discusses reviews of the field, which criticize staff structures and roles. This paper constitutes a valuable introduction to the issues of professionalization facing the informal learning sector.

Carl G. Glickman, *Leadership for Learning: How to Help Teachers Succeed,* (Alexandria, VA: Association for Supervision and Curriculum Development, 2002). Building on the framework defined by Charlotte Danielson, Carl Glickman discusses "structures for classroom assistance--clinical supervision, peer coaching, critical friends, and action research groups; formats for observations--frameworks for teaching, open-ended questionnaires, and samples of student work; and approaches to working directly with teachers--directive, collaborative and nondirective."

Jean Lave and Etienne Wenger, *Situated Learning: Legitimate Peripheral Participation* (Cambridge, UK: Cambridge University Press, 1991). Lave and Wenger examine learning not as "the reception of factual knowledge or information," but as "a process of participation in communities of practice."

Lynn Uyen Tran and Heather King, "The Professionalization of Museum Educators: The Case in Science Museums," *Museum Management and Curatorship* 22, no. 2 (2007):129-147. Tran and King use the sociological discourse on professions to scrutinize the professionalization process of museum education. They argue that professionalization provides a route to greater respect and recognition for museum educators; however, this field needs to identify a theoretically derived body of knowledge to underpin the nature of its professional preparation and practice.

ORGANIZATIONAL LEADERSHIP: GETTING STARTED RESOURCES

Also critical to the success of museum education leaders is a strong grasp of the latest concepts in **organizational leadership**. Many of the previous articles cite the most innovative literature on the topic, but we have included a few others that focus on the specifics of perennially difficult leadership challenges such as contract negotiations, communication, sustaining new cultures and maintaining resonance.

Lee G. Bolman and Terrance E. Deal, *Reframing Organizations: Artistry, Choice, and Leadership* (San Francisco, CA: Jossey-Bass Publications, 4th ed., 2008). A best-selling book since its first printing in 1984, *Reframing Organizations* has been updated with new examples from the private and nonprofit sectors. Bolman and Deal examine organizations through four frames: the structural frame, the human resources frame, the political frame, and the symbolic frame.

Richard E. Boyatzis and Annie McKee, *Resonant Leadership* (Boston, MA: Harvard Business School Press, 2005). "Boyatzis and McKee provide a practical framework for how leaders can create and sustain resonance in their relationships, their teams, and their organizations." They show how the concepts of mindfulness, hope and compassion have "proven implications for the practice of leadership, invoking the physiological and psychological changes that enable leaders to overcome the negative effects of chronic stress."

Yrjo Engestrom and David Middleton, eds., *Cognition and Communication at Work* (Boston, MA: Cambridge University Press, 1998). "This book brings together contributions from researchers within various social science disciplines who seek to redefine the methods and topics that constitute the study of work. They investigate work activity in ways that do not reduce it to a "psychology" of individual cognition or to a "sociology" of societal structures and communication. A key theme in the material is the relationship between theory and practice. Mindful practices and communicative interaction are examined as situated issues at work in the reproduction of communities of practice in a variety of settings including: courts of law, computer software design, the piloting of airliners, the coordination of air traffic control, and traffic management in underground railway systems."

Roger Fisher and William Ury, *Getting to YES: Negotiating Agreement Without Giving In*, 2nd ed. (New York: Penguin Books, 1991). *Getting to YES* offers a concise, step-by-step, proven strategy for coming to mutually acceptable agreements in every sort of conflict . . . *Getting to YES* tells you how to separate the people from the problem; focus on interests, not positions; work together to create options that will satisfy both parties; and negotiate successfully with people who are more powerful, refuse to play by the rules, or resort to "dirty tricks."

CHANGE LEADERSHIP: GETTING STARTED RESOURCES

The last and most important section of resources is focused on building skills in **change leadership**. Change is hard. Ask anyone who has tried to quit smoking or lose weight. We start down a new path, full of hope and energy and with a vision of the future only to despair and revert back to the old ways of doing things when we encounter the first or second barrier. The references below help us to understand why organizations are not quick to change and why individuals have such a difficult time sustaining change. The references provide frameworks for engaging in the kind of leadership necessary to guide museum education into the future.

Michael Fullan, *The Six Secrets of Change: What the Best Leaders Do to Help Their Organizations Survive and Thrive* (San Francisco, CA: John Wiley & Sons, Inc. 2008). "In this book Fullan explores essential lessons for business and public sector leaders for surviving and thriving in today's complex environment. He draws on his acclaimed work in bringing about large-scale and substantial change in education reform in both public school systems and universities, as well as engaging in major initiatives internationally."

Tony Wagner, Robert Kegan, et al., *Change Leadership: A Practical Guide to Transforming Our Schools* (San Francisco, CA: John Wiley & Sons, Inc. 2006). The Change Leadership Group at the Harvard School of Education offers a new systemic change framework specifically geared toward education. Their framework enables organizational and individual change to occur and be sustained over time, leading toward continuous and transformational improvement in school settings.

Notes

1. Mr. Schatz is Vice President for Education at the Pacific Science Center in Seattle, Washington and author of "My Essential Booklist for Museum Educators Wearing Many Hats," *The Journal of Museum Education*, 31, no. 3 (Fall 2006): 234.

Correction

Dear Readers,

The Spring 2009 issue of the *Journal of Museum Education* featured an article titled "Impact of the National History Day in Ohio, Program on Students' Performances: Pilot Evaluation Project" by Giuseppe Monaco, Bo Lu, and Megan Wood. The figure "Rubric to Evaluate Critical Thinking" as printed on page 93 should have included a final column titled "Integrating New Perspectives." The column and its data was inadvertently left out of the original version. The corrected figure appears below.

The Editor

Figure 1. Rubric To Evaluate Critical Thinking

Garrison proposed five stages of critical thinking:
· Identifying a problem
· Defining the problem
· Exploring ways to deal with it
· Applying one of the strategies to the problem
· Integrating new perspectives
· For each of the steps, we evaluate the baseline and the progression during the discussion along the below-reported scale (from low to high or vice-versa).

Scale	Steps of Critical Thinking					
	Observation	Defining the problem	Exploring			Integrating New Perspectives
			Variety of Sources	Students' evaluation of credibility	Differentiation between primary and secondary sources	
Low	Recognize details of the picture (i.e., boys, no shoes)	Recognize the events without factual information (making up)	Only one	"Sounds right" "A lot of hits"	Little or no understanding	Recognition of connection without factual information
Medium	Defining the scene (i.e., child labor)	Recognize the events with factual information	More than one	My Professor told me because...	Under standing of the differences	Recognition of connection with factual information
High	Extrapolate and put in historical context (i.e., depression era)	Elaborate on the context of the events	Combination and relation among more than two sources.	Reasons behind the selection process	Using both and explain why and how	Historical connection/ taking advantage of learning from the past

Reasons behind the selection process
Using both and explain why and how
Historical connection/ taking advantage of learning from the past

For Product Safety Concerns and Information please contact our EU
representative GPSR@taylorandfrancis.com Taylor & Francis Verlag GmbH,
Kaufingerstraße 24, 80331 München, Germany

Printed and bound by CPI Group (UK) Ltd, Croydon, CR0 4YY
11/04/2025
01843992-0015